Early Scottish Gardens

SHEILA MACKAY

Early Scottish Gardens

A WRITER'S ODYSSEY

POLYGON
AT EDINBURGH

Frontispiece:

NORTHFIELD HOUSE

Garden tools at the entrance to Northfield House, Prestonpans, Midlothian.
The lintel inscription reads 'Except the Lord Bvlds In Vain Bvlds Man'.

© The Royal Commission on the Ancient and Historical Monuments of Scotland.

EARLY
SCOTTISH
GARDENS

© Sheila Mackay, 2001

POLYGON AT EDINBURGH
An imprint of Edinburgh University Press Ltd
22 George Square, Edinburgh

A CIP Record for this book is
available from the British Library

ISBN 0 7486 6254 5 (paperback)

Designed by Mark Blackadder

Typeset in Ehrhardt

Printed and bound in Great Britain by Bookcraft Ltd, Midsomer Norton, Bath

Contents

COLOUR PLATES

For copyright and acknowledgement details,
please see pages 215–16.

Wagner Carpet

Dean House Panels: *Sight Personified*,
Hearing Personified and *Taste Personified*

Northfield House

Celestial Ceiling at Cullen

Bee-Boles at Kellie Castle

Wall of Planetary Deities, Edzell

Traquair Embroidery

Esther Inglis

Inscription, Earlshall

Blairadam

The Pineapple

Yester House

Blair Castle

Lion: House of Dun

FOR STEPHEN
AND ARIANE

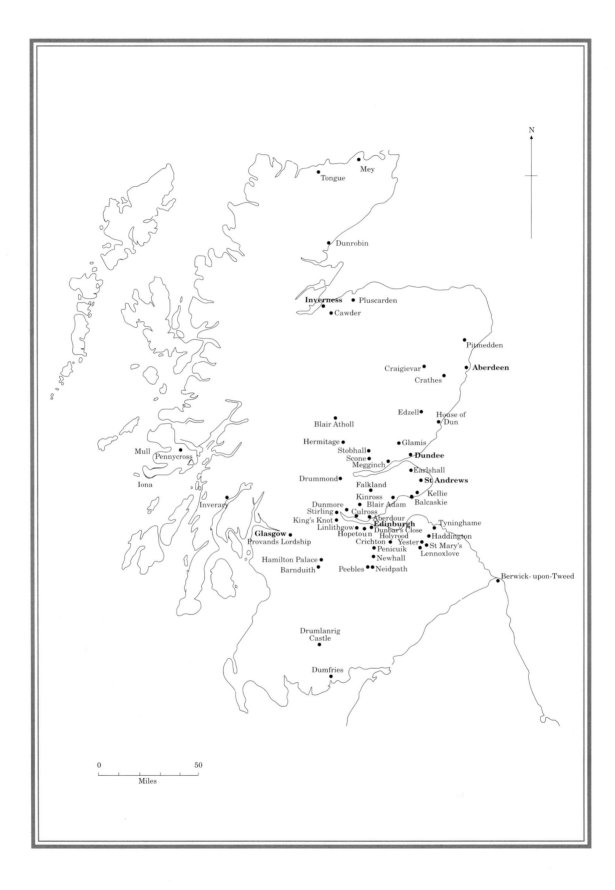

N

Mey
Tongue

Dunrobin

Inverness • Pluscarden
•Cawder

Pitmedden

Craigievar • **Aberdeen**
Crathes

Edzell • House of
Dun

Blair Atholl

Hermitage • Glamis
Stobhall **Dundee**
Scone
Megginch

Mull
Pennycross Drummond Earlshall
St Andrews
Iona Falkland Kellie
Kinross Balcaskie
Dunmore Blair Adam
Inverary Stirling Culross
King's Knot Aberdour
Linlithgow **Edinburgh** Tyninghame
Hopetoun Dunbar's Close Haddington
Glasgow Holyrood
Provands Lordship Crichton Yester St Mary's
Penicuik Lennoxlove
Hamilton Palace • Newhall
Barnduith Peebles •Neidpath Berwick- upon-Tweed

Drumlanrig
Castle

Dumfries

0   50
Miles

Preface

What did early Scottish gardens look like? How did these gardens relate to the house and how did passing time affect their development? Where did the plant stock come from: herbs, shrubs, annuals and perennials from the thistle to the rose? Often, looking out from the windows of Renaissance and Baroque houses while working on a previous book about Scottish interiors, I had asked myself these questions.

Surely gardens matched the richly embellished interiors of Scots aristocrats and merchants, particularly after the Reformation? Furthermore, given Scotland's vibrant trading network with Europe and the steady procession abroad of our aristocrats, diplomats and scholars since medieval times, our gardens must have kept up with equivalent European designs? Evocative and tantalising remains of 'missing gardens', such as earthworks, stone walls, doocots, date stones, terracing, traceries of paths, sundials, a few ancient yews, and gardens themselves – Culross, Edzell, Pitmedden, Kinross and all the others – fired my imagination, until, at last, I was ready to set out on my exploration.

To my surprise, I soon discovered in British garden histories overwhelmingly dismissive, vague or contradictory references to Scottish-designed landscapes before the eighteenth century. For example:

> From Scotland travellers' tales of the half-century after the Restoration continue to tell of a rough and hard way of life … the equivalent of the smaller type of English manor house or parsonage with it often productive and interesting garden scarcely existed;
>
> Or: in Scotland gardening seems to have been little developed;

Details of private gardens and properties not in the care of Historic Scotland or The National Trust for Scotland may be listed in the annual publication *Scotland's Garden Scheme*. Some are open to the public all year round or occasionally under the scheme's Open Days; others are strictly private or open for viewing by appointment only.

And: there are early records of orchards and vineyards – though in Scotland the fruit was apparently of poor quality.

Challenging assumptions including these examples rang in my ears. What about Bishop Leslie's description of the 'orchardes, and fruitful gairdings' of Morayshire in 1578 and the 'gentimenis places and gret palices' of Fife; and Sir William Brereton's discovery in 1635 between Dunbar and Edinburgh of 'very many seats of the nobles and found good apple and other fruit trees, walnuts and sycamores'?

Evidently the time had come to place the evidence for early Scottish gardens in a *European*, rather than an Anglocentric context. This was my starting point.

My most significant discovery along the way was the first representation of a formal garden in Scottish art (c.1580): the Dean House panel, part of a painted ceiling rescued from an Edinburgh chateau and now displayed at the Museum of Scotland. The delightful painting depicts Taste personified as a Muse, sipping from a goblet as she sits beside an ornamental lake and garden. Unequivocally, the panel conveys the message that *before the end of the sixteenth century* aspiring

Dean House Panels:
Sight personified (c.1580) with Edinburgh Castle and the Royal Park.

Opposite, top:
Taste personified (c.1580) beside a formal garden and a lake.

Opposite, below:
Hearing personified (c.1580).

Reprinted by permission of the Trustees of the National Museums of Scotland.

Scots required elaborate gardens to match houses and interiors that reflected their status, wealth and sense of self-esteem.

Connections, clues and waymarks accumulated as my search progressed. Another important clue emerged to back up my supposition that Scotland kept up with the rest of Europe in garden design. On the one hand I read that Scotland had no gardens to speak of before Union. Yet I also read: 'as early as the 1700s a sizable emigration of Scots gardeners crossed the Border' to seek work on English estates. And I wondered: *where had these gardeners come from if there had been no gardens to speak of in Scotland?*

I have suggested in the book imaginary gardens for the sixteenth-century calligrapher, Esther Inglis, and for George Jamesone, the seventeenth-century portrait painter, and have 'redesigned' the ground of the Pleasaunce at Edzell Castle, Forfarshire, in light of contemporary European developments, in an attempt to demonstrate that in the field of Scottish garden history more happened, earlier and far more dramatically than we have realised. The colour section of the book vividly portrays, step-by-step, Scotland keeping up with the rest of Europe in garden design and interior decoration: in the Renaissance Dean House panels and the Cullen Celestial Ceiling, for example, and on, through Edzell Castle Pleasaunce to Blairadam, the landscape style of Yester and 'Improvement' and tree-planting on a massive scale at Blair Castle.

Scottish members of the Garden History Society have for many years produced important and interesting papers in their journal. One of them is writing an eagerly awaited history of gardens in Scotland with the backing of Historic Scotland. In the mean time, my book is intended to be a stepping stone over a much smaller river and I hope it will encourage readers to make their own distinctive maps and undertake their own explorations.

The National Trust for Scotland has taken an imaginative lead in recreating many Scottish gardens, including Culross Palace Garden, Pitmedden Great Garden and Kellie Castle garden, and in preserving picturesque landscapes such as the Hermitage, all of which I have visited. Historic Scotland looks after our most ancient sites, including Arthur's Seat and the Royal Park of Holyroodhouse where I began my journey, and has in its keeping the jewel of early gardens, the

Pleasaunce at Edzell Castle. Reconstructions of early seventeenth-century gardens include St Mary's Pleasance, Haddington, the garden at Provand's Lordship, Glasgow, and that at Dunbar's Close in Edinburgh's Royal Mile. In these places the visitor experiences virtual reality. The design is felicitous, birds delight in flitting and nesting there, the plants smell as they did four centuries ago, and, in at least one of these recent gardens, additional pleasure is to be had from the knowledge that, but for the generosity and determination of the Trust that created it, the site would have been developed commercially.

I had help across my stepping stones – ten passages between 1500 and 1750, from Arthur's Seat to the Hermitage – and acknowledge my gratitude and warmest thanks as follows. Hugh Cheape drew my attention to the Dean House panels; John Gifford saw an early synopsis of my book and encouraged me to take it further; Nicola Carr commissioned the book for Polygon at Edinburgh; the work of garden historians, and in particular papers written by Fiona Jamieson and Priscilla Minay, added immeasurably to the text; Mary Rutherford first told me about the Beaton medical kindred of the west coast; Mary Beith offered wise comments and suggested additions to the text; and the enthusiastic and unfailing assistance of the staff at the Royal Botanical Garden, Edinburgh, and at the Scottish Library of Edinburgh Public Libraries helped to make my venture a great pleasure.

Sing of the gardens, O my heart,
of Shiraz and Isfahan
As if glass domes had placed them
out of reach forever

Rainer Maria Rilke
Sonnets to Orpheus

CHAPTER I

Arthur's Seat and the Royal Park

PINKY-WHITE YARROW, STARRY WHITE HEATH BEDSTRAW,

FEATHERY GOLDEN LADY'S BEDSTRAW, PEA-LIKE PURPLE MILK-VETCH,

BELL HEATHER, COMMON SORREL AND SHEEP'S SORREL

The sun soars free of the summit towards mid-morning. It illuminates the green sward of the Royal Park of Holyrood and defines the craggy knolls of Arthur's Seat, a highland microcosm spread beyond the double windows of my room. A great medieval household on the move comes into imaginary view, that of a knight of James IV, perhaps, slipping and slithering over the rocky Gutted Haddie, returning from Neidpath Castle in Peeblesshire. An impressive procession of several hundred, its important members colourful and decorative on horseback, the hodden-clad serfs and their children on foot beside packhorses outrageously laden with the possessions of the household. Slowly and steadily the procession clears Hunter's Bog, mercifully dry after a summer drought, and begins the short descent towards Holyrood Palace. There the retainers set up their lord's interior with plate, jewels, tapestries, table coverings, chests, beds, musical instruments, carpenter's tools, mass-books, sacramental vessels, cooking utensils, roasting spits, pots and pans. And gardening tools?

Suddenly my winter dark room is briefly bright and I know the time has come to put the reference books, notes and papers into the filing cabinet and begin my own journey. For long enough I have wondered: how did gardens evolve in Scotland? What did early gardens look like and how did they develop, and where did the plant stock come from, violets and carnations and all the hardy annuals from the thistle to the rose? My mind is filled with factual information, only it has become clear – there is no definitive story entitled 'how gardens grew in Scotland'. I must set off in my own directions, along selected paths, knowing that others who follow me will make their own detours and discoveries, feeling challenged as I do by statements I have read more than once to the effect that 'there were no gardens to speak of in Scotland before the eighteenth century'.

The arrival of the household brought the fortified towerhouses to life, as the rooms filled with people and gear. They had left behind, more or less empty, the fortified structures that belonged to the lord, scattered many miles apart, in Scotland, on the outskirts of civilisation. The blueprints for these structures evolved from the broch, that uniquely Scottish circular form of wood and stone that both sheltered and defended. Now, 2000 years later, castles and smaller fortified

Wagner Carpet: richly coloured and ornately designed Islamic garden carpets depict earthly enclosed gardens as a reflection of gardens in the paradise to come.

Glasgow Museums: Burrell Collection, reproduced by permission.

8

structures, within a ditch and high-towered walls, triangular, rectangular or polygonal according to the landscape of the site, emulated the architectural influences of rich and populous medieval Europe. These single stone towers, 'fortalices' set in small courts or 'barmkins', included the lord's house. And their owners had obligations: to administer local government, to raise fighting men for the army or 'host' or for local skirmishes, and to maintain courtly ceremony. Their households of people from all walks of life were large; their lives revolved around the great hall, the heart of the castle. And were there gardens to speak of?

For long enough I have looked out of windows of houses whose history is more or less documented and wondered about the garden ground. Now it's time to make real the chaos of information gleaned from books on plants, books on gardens, extracts from the Garden History Society's newsletter and the Royal Commission's *Inventory of Designed Landscapes in Scotland*, copies of old maps, drawings of flowers – and as I gather everything into a neat pile, the cleared carpet displays its pattern to me as if for the first time. The design represents an ancient oriental garden in shades of purple, orange-red and gold, an early designed landscape of water channels, lilies, pomegranates, palms, arabesques, fish and gazelles. An earthly paradise. The first map of my journey.

I fret about the scope of what I have taken on as I scurry across the open flatland behind the Palace of Holyroodhouse towards Hunter's Bog, my scarf well wrapped against the bitter cold. Now I am on my way. But in winter, the worst time of year for a journey, when I had been waiting for the spring? Today is St Brigid's Day, the first of February; it's cold enough for snow. A day of deep dormancy when Brigid, the Celtic Minerva, is said to have spread her cloak over the ground to create both darkness and protective warmth. A time of dormancy for seeds and bulbs, a time to draw energy for spring growth. Seagulls bask at the edge of St Margaret's Loch, their backs tinged Reckitt's blue in the brightness. The jagged outline of the summit above looks drawn against the sky with a thick nibbed pen. It is bleak up here alright, the ground denuded of foliage and peppered with rabbit droppings and I think, when a journey begins who knows what might be lost or gained, but I am happy enough to have been led here by the hand of fate, or whichever goddess it was – Brigid, perhaps? – who got me off the chair in my cosy room and up to this high and lonely place.

Here I wait and wander the high reaches of Arthur's Seat, blowing into knitted gloves, stamping my feet against the cold every time I stop to consider which criss-crossing path to take. Monks came here, the Stewart kings hunted here, Queen Mary staged a festival here, the keeper of the physic garden that preceded the Royal Botanic Garden of Edinburgh gathered native plants here. Suddenly it all falls into place. Unwittingly I have stumbled on the perfect place from which to start my search for significant gardens.

Schiehallion or Buchaille Etive Mor might have been my starting point, for in wild places like these, from foothills to treeline, you can still discover much of the native flora of Scotland, around 1500 species established by 3000 BC. The Royal Park and Arthur's Seat, formed by aeons of glacial and volcanic weathering, still host a variety of these native plants. As I climb higher and higher, I realise that this particular hill, surrounded by the civilising city, has advantages over any remote ben that might have made my starting point. From Pulpit Hill or Windy Gowl, or any of Arthur's Seat's high places, you see swards and structures that send the imagination spinning from the retreat of the last Ice Age to the eighteenth century. Prehistoric cultivation terraces, best seen in the afternoon light, the runrigs of early pastoralists (the first people to introduce plants), the ancient St Anthony's Chapel above St Margaret's Loch (monks introduced plants and designed gardens). Looking south in the direction of Selkirk brings Soutra Hill to mind, where an Augustinian order retained 230 plant species in the fourteenth century. Monks and monarchs, and their herbariums and garden landscapes are well represented from the vantage point high above Salisbury Crags, as are sixteenth- and seventeenth-century Scots whose gardens grew round their towerhouses, several hundred within a mile or two of Holyrood Park.

Strips of tenement and townhouse gardens, called 'lands' or 'rigs', can be imagined too, ribbing out from the backbone of the Royal Mile at the Canongate. These gardens, with parterres, knots and kitchen gardens, had been established well before Gordon of

Rothiemay published his 'Bird's Eye View of Edinburgh' in 1647. Most of the sites of 'around one hundred' chateaux or towerhouses the Duc de Rohan claimed to have counted from Edinburgh Castle in 1600 are visible from Arthur's Seat. Dean House and its policies were situated where the Dean Cemetery spreads near Queensferry Road today. From the painted ceilings of that chateau we have the most important recent find in Scottish garden history: the first representation of a garden in Scottish painting (c.1580), now on display at the Museum of Scotland.

Looking north-west across the Firth of Forth I anticipate travelling to Culross where Sir George Bruce had constructed a fine mansion and gardens by 1604. George Bruce was one of many merchants made wealthy in the economic boom at the end of the sixteenth century, a member of a rising 'middling sort' (traders, feuars and the new professionals) who required homes and garden grounds worthy of their new-found status and affluence. In this period, with the court gone to London, the royal holdings declined even as private building works boomed.

1604 is also the date of the Pleasaunce at Edzell, Forfar, whose significance is impossible to exaggerate, and whose exploration will form the climax of my journey. Much closer to hand, I am overlooking

Enlarged detail from James Gordon of Rothiemay's 'Bird's Eye View of Edinburgh' (1647) showing the gardens surrounding the Palace of Holyroodhouse and the private gardens behind the tenements and townhouses of the Canongate.

Courtesy of Edinburgh City Libraries.

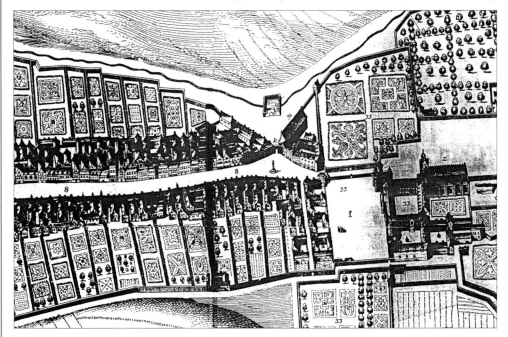

the site of the first physic garden, St Anne's Yard, the sward behind the Palace of Holyroodhouse whose keeper, James Sutherland, worked alongside the great Baroque architect Sir William Bruce. To the east I can see the Bass Rock, the focal point of the axial path at Balcaskie near St Monans, Bruce's inspired house and landscape. Away to the north-west, Benartie Hill curves the horizon near Kinross House, Bruce's masterpiece, not far from Blairadam, William Adam's own home. To the west, the Forth Bridge indicates the nearby site of Hopetoun House, where both Bruce and Adam had a hand in designing the landscape as well as the house. Then, looking to the south-east, I imagine Yester House nestling under the Lammermuir Hills. The destruction of Yester's great formal garden in favour of English landscape style in the middle of the eighteenth century would be a sad ending to my journey. Yet there is a way out, along the inspired paths of the landowner, poet and dilettante, Sir John Clerk of Penicuik House, to search for the Grotto of his Elysium.

My travels and this book have the same intention: to rediscover our 'missing' gardens and to explore with a fresh eye the remnants of some early gardens that still exist. For too long we have lived without (and scarcely noticed the absence of) a vibrant facet of our cultural heritage: the most basic at that, considering that the very word 'culture' derives from the same root as 'cultivation'. We have been content to believe that after the Fall, in that faraway biblical land, gardens in Scotland scarcely existed until the seventeenth century. It cannot be stressed too often that British garden histories written this century have perpetuated the myth; only, after weeks of delving in many sources, I know it cannot be so – our early gardens simply went missing. Untended and undocumented, they fell into rack and ruin. Nevertheless I hope to demonstrate that from medieval times the evolution of gardens in Scotland kept pace with the rest of Europe, ideologically at least, and often in fact.

Michael Lynch has observed: 'Much of the best writing [about Scottish history] in the past generation has been taken up with showing that less happened, and less dramatically, than was once thought.' In the field of Scottish garden history the need now is to demonstrate that more happened, far more dramatically than we have been led to believe. And when you start discovering clues, it doesn't take long to realise it

must be so. A significant contributing factor to our cultural gap has been our reticence to set Scottish garden history within the dynamic social, political and cultural context that affects every other dimension of our history, that is, within a European, rather than an English context.

After venturing a little into monastic times, my journey and this book both begin at the opening of the sixteenth century. However, striding out on the bleak high reaches of Arthur's Seat, it is impossible to resist glancing over my shoulder even further back, into prehistory to discover the native flora.

The last Ice Age retreated 10 000 years ago, leaving behind modified landscapes like this one at Holyrood Park, scooping out earlier volcanic ashes to create hollows like the Dry Dam area (a relic from Carboniferous times, around 350 million years ago) where meadow pipits flit in spring, skylarks sing, owls hunt voles and kestrels wind-hover under the crags. The summit marks a vent of the old volcano above Pulpit Rock, formed from laval flow, while the Lang Row opposite was created by a different earlier flow from the volcanic vent now topped by Edinburgh Castle.

On Whinny Hill low-growing summer flowers, many of them natives established after the retreat of the ice, have adapted to thin soil: pinky-white yarrow, starry white heath bedstraw, feathery golden lady's bedstraw, pea-like purple milk-vetch, bell heather, common sorrel and sheep's sorrel.

On the far side of the Lion's Haunch beside the Queen's Drive different flowers grow in the lime-rich soil. Yellow rockrose, bloody cranesbill, spiky blue viper's bugloss and rockrose thrive in natural rock gardens; sandwort and garlic mustard swell verges of bramble, elder and hawthorn. Ragwort blooms on the walls with groundsel. Biting stonecrop, restharrow and bur chervil cover the ground.

A long time later, and long before there was any thought of enclosing ground for protective reasons, landscapes with good soil deposits, firth lands such as the Forth, the Tay and the Ness, were inhabited by hunter-gatherers who survived by collecting growing things. After that, the first European farmers arrived in Britain across the relatively recently flooded English Channel, bringing domesticated

animals and cereal mixtures containing seeds of the weeds that became the first artificially introduced plants. Eventually these incomers, the 'pastoralists', superseded the Stone Age gatherers. They cleared forests for arable crops and grazing animals to create the first 'artificial' heathlands and grasslands of Scotland so that by Bronze and Iron Age times, most components of the rural landscape as we know it had been established: hilly grassland, pastures, heaths and heathers on more acid soils, arable fields in wide river valleys, scrub, coppice woodland and sedgy fens.

This essentially human-made landscape echoed the natural open state that had existed after the Ice Age and before the forest took over, when the entire British countryside must have resembled an artfully landscaped garden with abundant plant species flourishing in light, warmth, moisture and increasingly fertile soil. In summer the lime-based Burren area of western Ireland and parts of the west coast of Scotland, like the island of Lismore, whose very name suggests 'great garden', retain flourishing *machairs* which reflect the abundant early native flora. After that almost all additions to the list of established native plants were deliberate or accidental introductions by man.

Holyrood Park and the volcanic relics of Arthur's Seat form a microcosm of landscape and history, named, according to legend, after King Arthur who held court here, but no one knows for certain. Apart from its summit, remote wildness is the most dramatic feature of the place. Up here you are well away from the city's throng and as I head towards home, faintly it comes back to me. A sunny day in summer, that ineffable smell of Scottish landscape, a sweet mix of earth, grasses, gorse and wildflowers blown on the breeze. Up the gorsey, grassy Dry Dam common knapweed grows with bramble, thistle and wood sage, recognisable from its yellow-green flower spikes and strange pungent smell, and I remember that James Sutherland included these plants with dozens of other natives in his 1683 catalogue of the plants that grew in his physic garden.

Up here, each geological feature belongs to an Edinburgh songline: Lion's Haunch, Hunter's Bog, Windy Gowl, Pulpit Rock and all the other evocations from Haggis Knowe to the Girnal and the Echoing Rocks. I have looked over my shoulder into the past. Now I

slope down an obvious path past Samson's Ribs where I am on future ground, since my journey's end has the date stamp 'around 1750'. After that, this most famous geological site in Scotland inspired James Hutton (1726–97) to write his *Theory of the Earth* and here Charles Darwin gathered rock samples when he was a student at Edinburgh University. Between the Seat and Salisbury Crags, a rockface formed by molten rock cooled into a sill and carved by Ice-Age erosion, brings me down to the Radical Road, a twisting path that evokes the 'landskips' of James Norie (1684–1757), the songs of Robert Burns and Sir Walter Scott's *The Heart of Midlothian* which describes the politically radical unemployed weavers who built this very road. Up here there is an unrivalled view of the city, Edinburgh Castle, and the Royal Mile constructed on its sloping glacial wedge, as well as the site of Scotland's Parliament building.

I see the building works going on in the fading light of a winter afternoon and it fills me with hope as I return to the fire, satisfied that a start has been made. Nothing clears the mind so well as a walk in the landscape and, at the very least, I have sketched out an itinerary in my mind. Arthur's Seat has disappeared into the darkness beyond the window but I shall return there again and again now that the place has revealed itself as a sort of touchstone, a direction indicator. And when I reinvent James Sutherland, digging up cranesbill for his physic garden somewhere near Hunter's Bog, I shall be half-way through my journey.

At the beginning of a book there is the first blank page
A garden begins as a patch of earth in an enclosed space
Sentences become paragraphs, paragraphs become pages
The gardener designs the plot, lays out paths, plants herbs, flowers and trees
The writer gathers information, makes connections, creates a style
The book takes form; the garden grows.

CHAPTER 2

Hidden Gardens

A GARDEN ENCLOSED IS MY SISTER, MY SPOUSE;

A SPRING SHUT UP, A FOUNTAIN SEALED

Monastic orders grew plants and seeds from Europe in their herbariums, mainly for their curative powers and sometimes for their religious symbolism. The highest of Britain's monastic sites is 17 miles south-east of Edinburgh on the windswept Border hills at Soutra, a main highway from England to Edinburgh and once an important invasion route. A healing well is believed to have affected the Augustinian order's decision to build a hospital here and a recent excavation claims to have uncovered evidence of over two hundred plant species with medical application, including exotic herbs and spices imported from abroad, such as pepper, ginger, nutmeg, cloves, frankincense and myrrh.

It's bitterly cold as I stand at the bleak site staring into the excavated foundations, summoning up the ghost of an apothecary monk concocting anaesthetics from available plants and seeds for urgent use in the grisly fourteenth-century Wars of Independence. Even in summer Soutra is an inhospitable place, famous for its fast-changing weather, and today, with snow forecast, my car is in sight, parked down on the road, ready for a quick getaway if necessary. Away over the snow-girt landscape, Edinburgh Castle and Arthur's Seat stand out as if drawn in charcoal.

Edward II stayed at the Soutra monastery with a retinue and army of 50 000 on his way to defeat at Bannockburn in 1314 and many of the wounded must have returned to be operated on and healed, or to die. The examination of 800-year-old medical waste excavated here showed that the Augustinian monks carried out vast numbers of operations and amputations. Opium poppy, flax and hemp (cannabis) were cultivated on the site and seeds of black henbane and hemlock, known ingredients of general anaesthetics, have been dated around 1320. Less dramatic herbal preparations have been identified too, such as tormentil, the yellow ground-hugging plant that grows profusely on these Border hills, cited in medieval recipes as good for 'slaying' worms. Although the monks grew and collected plants primarily for their healing and painkilling properties, some plants – juniper is an example – were also endowed with religious symbolism. Juniper berries and wood were burned in medieval hospitals to purify the air and sometimes as an inexpensive substitute for ceremonial incense. The berries, commonly used in the Middle Ages, have been found at Soutra with the deadly ergot fungus, known to cause catastrophic contraction of the uterus. Juniper is a uterine stimulant and the combination of ergot and juniper may have assisted both childbirth and abortions, a conjecture strengthened by the discovery of bone fragments from a fetus at the site. Juniper, customarily grown as a bush at the centre of monastic herb gardens to represent the Tree of Life, finds an echo in the centrally placed fountains of later secular gardens.

On a gentler note, I recall the story of William Rufus's visit to the gardens of the nuns at Romsey, hoping to catch a glimpse of Edith of Scotland, heiress to the Saxon line. The princess, dressed as a nun, remained concealed, though Rufus's disappointment may have been ameliorated by the sight and smell of roses, lilies and other flowering plants he found in the Romsey garden.

The monks of Scotland's monastic foundations gleaned their knowledge of the power of plants through their own dispensaries, from medical encyclopedias such as the first-century AD *De Materia Medica,* compiled by Pliny the Elder's physician, Dioscorides, from laboriously hand-copied herbals and, later, from the Arabic medicine being taught at Salerno, Bologna and Montpellier. In the seventeenth century, Robert Sibbald, one of the founders of the Edinburgh physic garden, would study at Montpellier. Dioscorides' encyclopedia lists the cultivation and uses of 500 specimens, including plants the Romans and Visigoths introduced to the West from India, China and Arabia by way of Egypt, Greece, Rome and the Byzantine empire. By the eleventh century bulbous plants, bay, tamarisk, pines, olives, artichokes, figs, cypresses, dates, violets, roses, pomegranates, sugar cane, ginger and mulberries were only a small selection of introductions to Europe, meticulously recorded. Supplementary lists to Dioscorides' encyclo-pedia were regularly published by early physicians and others who participated in botanical expeditions. The encyclopedia was translated into several languages and distributed throughout Europe until the sixteenth century, when the invention of printing encouraged the publication of many books, ancient and new, about horticulture and garden design.

In the ages before printing, a trained memory was vitally important to orators (lay and ecclesiastical), to storytellers, scholars,

poets and others dependent on the spoken word. A sound grasp of the techniques of the art allowed orators to deliver long speeches from memory with unfailing accuracy and to repeat oral history. The art of memory evolved through the Middle Ages when Augustine declared that it was one of the three powers of the soul: Memory, Understanding and Will, the image of the Trinity in man. In its early development Quintillian (c. AD 35–98) gave a clear expression of the art of memory devised by Simonides the Greek:

> In order to form a series of places in memory (which can be visited and re-visited if necessary in the course of a speech or performance) a building, for example, might be remembered, as spacious and varied as possible – the forecourt, the living room, bedrooms and parlours, the statues, ornaments that decorate the room. Memorised images of the speech are then placed in the imagination on the places which have been memorized in the building.

Early memory images included walled gardens.

> We have to think of the ancient orator [ ] moving in his imagination through his memory building [or garden] whilst he is making his speech, drawing from the memorized places the images he has placed on them. The method ensures that the points are remembered in the right order, since the order is fixed by the sequence of places in the building,

writes Frances Yates in her stirring book, *The Art of Memory*. Each room, each object in the room, served as a prompt for what the speaker had to say next.

What has the art of memory to do with gardens? An art which uses contemporary architecture for its memory places and contemporary imagery for its images will have its classical, Gothic and Renaissance periods like every other art … including gardening. And formal early gardens, divided into 'rooms', acted as *aides-mémoire*. In Rossellius' *Thesaurus of Artificial Memory* (Venice, 1579) paradise is depicted as an enclosed garden, an 'arbor vitae', with a central mount

and planted beds, and Romberch's memory system based on the alphabet (Venice, 1533) includes gardening implements.

Augustinian Soutra has been a detour on my way to the Benedictine Pluscarden Abbey where a Frenchman, Guillaume Lubias, is credited with designing the landscape in 1540. I am happy enough to drive away from the biting winds of Soutra that seem to swirl with groans and cries as well as the smell of incense and beeswax candles, and I wonder as I drive back to Edinburgh how monastic gardens might have looked in more fertile, sheltered places such as Pluscarden in Morayshire. Studying a map of the Highlands, I see that Cawdor Castle is not far from the abbey. The Pluscarden monks and the thanes of Cawdor might well have exchanged plants. Throughout Europe, seeds, cuttings and dried specimens of indigenous species, vigorously exchanged between the monasteries and the fortified homes of the monarchy and aristocracy to which they were linked, built up plant stock with vital medical properties as well as symbolic significance within their evolving garden landscapes.

All I know of Pluscarden is that long before they decided to make a foundation here, a Vasculian order from Burgundy sent a hermit to live in a cell and report on the lie of the lands in the great swathe of the Moray Firth, where the Black Burn runs between the Monaughty and Dallas forests. His report was favourable and Pluscarden Priory, founded in 1230, became linked in a fertile triangle with two others: Beauly and Ardchattan. Once established, the monks grew plants in their French-style enclosed grounds, for medicinal purposes in accordance with their duty to tend the sick, the poor and the aged.

The monks were not alone in healing the sick with herbal medicine. There existed in the Gaelic world, from c.1300 to c.1700, medical kindreds with just that aim. One of these kindred was distributed throughout the entire west coast, with an outpost on the north coast (Melness), two near the Black Isle and one near contemporary Dundee. Originally called the MacBeths, by the mid-sixteenth century they were known as the Beatons in non-Gaelic circles. Hector Boece (1465–1536) remarked on this kin-based medical profession's knowledge of 'the nature of every herbe that growis in thay cuntreis,

and curis all maner of maledyis thairwith'. The Beatons tended herbal gardens, or physic gardens. The remains of one at least, at Pennycross, Mull, can still be seen, and it has been suggested that the *hortus medicus* or physic garden established in Edinburgh (1670) 'was no more than that at Pennycross writ large'.

From the beginning of the twelfth century the designed landscapes of the French monasteries with which they were familiar, are likely to have acted as important patterns in the monks' minds' eyes, memory images for their modest Scottish priory gardens.

According to a contemporary source Clairvaux Abbey in Burgundy contained:

> wide level ground; here there [is an] orchard, with a great many different fruit trees, quite like a small wood. It is close to the infirmary and is very comforting to the brothers, providing a wide promenade for those who want to walk, and a pleasant resting place for those who prefer to rest. Where the orchard leaves off, the garden begins, divided into several beds or (still better) cut up by little canals …. The water fulfils the double purpose of nourishing the fish and watering the vegetables.

In that contemporary literary observation of Clairvaux Abbey garden lies several clues to the influences at play in the evolution of monastic gardens and the aristocratic gardens of Europe that emulated them. First, there was the immeasurable influence of Rome. The early Church in Italy and the Hellenic world had settled into original Roman villa sites and perpetuated the enclosed gardens it found there, laid out with cloisters, pilasters, covered walks, geometric paths and beds where plants with medicinal application were grown. The symbolism of the hidden garden within a garden reaches back to the Song of Solomon:

> A garden enclosed is my sister, my spouse;
> a spring shut up, a fountain sealed.

Later, northern European sites – Clairvaux Abbey's garden, for example – demonstrated features of early Egyptian and Moorish gardens. A garden outwith the orchard, its raised beds divided by paths

Earthly paradise: an
enclosed orchard garden
with a central canal and
fish pond, flanked with
willows and cypresses.
Citrus trees underplanted
with poppies, lilies and
narcissi perfume the air.

MS Or 338.f.110, by permission
of the British Library.

or canals containing fish and watering vegetables, its design is similar to
the richly coloured Wagner carpet that can be seen at the Burrell
Collection, Glasgow.

Often I walk across Holyrood Park to stand at St Anthony's Chapel,
waiting for signs of growth on the hills. Early travellers were impressed
by the fertility of the Lowlands and Morayshire but remarked on the
bleak, barren Highlands. There was a long period of exceptionally cold
weather after the Reformation and before the 1707 Union when cold
northern and easterly winds intensified the chill of winter and rain

drenched the stormy summers. The past few years, including this one,
have followed a similar pattern and winter has enveloped the Highlands
in snow. The roads are impassable, the lochs frozen over. Dormancy
deepens and I have to postpone my trip to Morayshire until the spring,
until the day comes at last when the first skylarks singing above the
gorse in the Royal Park of Holyrood remind me of James I
(1394–1437), imprisoned at Windsor, where he wrote 'The Kingis
Quhair', a poem that refers to a nightingale's clear song in the garden
beneath his prison walls with its allees and arbours. It seemed both an
earthly and a heavenly garden to the King waking in bed alone:

> Now was there maid fast by the towris wall
> A gardyn fair, and in the corneris set
> Ane herber grene with wandis long and small   [pailings]
> Railit about; and so with treis set
> Was all the place, and hawthorn hegis knet,
> That lyf was non walking there forby,
> That myght within scarce ony wight aspy.
>
> So thik the bewis and the leves grene   [boughs]
> Beschadit all the aleyes that there were,
> And myddis every herber myght be sene
> The scharp grene suete jenepere,
> Growing so fair with branches here and there,
> That, as it semyt to a lyfe without,
> The bewis spread the arbor all about;
>
> And on the small grene twistis sat   [branches]
> The lytill swete nyghtingale, and song
> So loud and clere the ympnis consecrat   [hymns]

Formal gardens of the kind the King describes in his poem had become
an established element of cultural consciousness by the Middle Ages,
when Scottish soldiers, students, scholars and traders tramped the
roads of Europe and left their mark. They returned home as propa-
gandists for the cultures they had experienced, and for the gardens they
had visited. Thousands of Scots settled in Europe, and Europeans

settled here (for example, Normans after the Conquest, Flemish, Germans and Dutch in and around our eastern ports in the Middle Ages, Italian and French craftsmen and gardeners in the Renaissance). Our culture had a European context. Plant stock entered our ports, and travellers brought back interesting specimens to Scotland as early as anywhere else.

At last the Highland snow has retreated to the summits and I drive north on the A95, appreciating a slight lifting of Brigid's cloak to reveal snowdrops and pussy willows in the woods. Lubias might well have sailed from France to Aberdeen, or one of the smaller eastern ports, Stonehaven or Montrose, and travelled on horseback along rough Highland tracks until he found Pluscarden. Wheeled transport was uncommon and carriages were almost unheard of in his day, though carts were used in the larger towns. (Mary, Queen of Scots, caused a stir when she imported a carriage from France in 1561.) Heavy loads were transported by boat on navigable stretches or moved short distances overland on rollers or horse-drawn sledges. Scotland was easily accessible by sea – the North Sea heaved with interchange – but travel in the interior was a different matter. Lubias's journey to the Abbey garden, over squelching mosses, slaps and styles, past hovels where the rural poor lived under the same roof as their animals, is likely to have been memorable. Did he break his journey with the thanes at Cawdor Castle or, if he sailed into Scotland by way of the Tay, at Megginch? Megginch Castle near Dundee stands in the fertile Carse of Gowrie, known as the 'Garden of Scotland'. The estate is thought to have been an early Christian monastery and the first planting is attributed to monks, as long as a thousand years ago; a yew hedge has become the four ancient yews that mark the boundary of the Terraced Garden. One, over 72 feet, is probably the highest yew in Scotland. By 1460 'the tower and fortalice of Megginich' is recorded and a wing was added in 1575, during Scotland's first 'building boom'.

The castles of the nobility (whose ancestors had received titles and privileges since the thirteenth century in exchange for raising armies in times of strife) had been contained within constructed enclosures (with woods, fruit trees, fishponds, doocots and the like) since the thirteenth century. It is likely that the lord's house at the

centre of a settlement had a *hortus conclusus* in the manner of monastic gardens – a garden sanctuary, planted out with herbs and 'simple' plants or natives with woods beyond. Characteristically, in other parts of Europe, plants and herbs were set in a herbarium within a larger *hortus conclusus*, and beyond the *hortus conclusus*, a place of safety and privacy protected by abbey, castle or tower, lay landscaped parks of woods and orchards. In addition to providing shelter for the enclosed garden, these trees served the fruit and timber trade which was highly profitable in fifteenth-century Scotland.

By 1454, the 6th Thane had built Cawdor Castle around an ancient hawthorn (carbon-dated to 1375). A portion of medieval wall can still be found in today's Walled Garden. They may also have constructed a courtyard herber such as the one shown in a Flemish miniature (1460) by the Master of Margaret of York where gardeners work with spades and wooden rakes in raised beds divided by paths. A recollection of the garden walls at Stobhall by James IV dates the garden there between 1458 and 1513.

The late fifteenth century embraced the cult of chivalry when the courtyard castle supplanted the fortified towerhouse as an expression of the possibility of a more leisured style of living among the Europolitan elite. James, Master of Douglas, who had been a student at Cologne, became highly regarded as an exemplar of chivalry after his performance in a tournament with knights from Burgundy at Stirling in 1449. William, 8th Earl of Douglas, who put on a brilliant show during a pilgrimage to Rome in 1450, is said to have kept a near-royal Scottish court and hung the walls of his noble halls with richly embroidered tapestries. Scots nobles held court in great halls, vigorously embellished with carved stone armorials, lest there be any doubt about their status. Many had travelled to Italy and other parts of Europe where tapestries similarly insulated rooms in winter but also recalled the pleasures of the summer garden in a riot of botanically accurate flowers. These nobles had a taste for chivalric romances and supported the foundation of collegiate churches in the middle of the century. They were well-educated people who must have been familiar with medieval literature such as the *Roman de la Rose*, in which the walled garden represents the Garden of Eden, so firmly rooted in Christian imagery. The court poet, William Dunbar (c.1460–1520), was in contact with both Lydgate and

Chaucer, both of whom extolled the *Romance of the Rose*. A valance from a bed formerly at Balloch (Taymouth Castle), now in the Burrell Collection, shows scenes of Adam and Eve in Paradise and their expulsion from the Garden of Eden on either side of the Campbell and Ruthven arms of the owners of the tapestry.

But these gardens of the imagination also reflected reality. Scottish nobles, as guests of foreign courts on their tours abroad, must have seen works like the illuminated Cocharelli manuscript (late fourteenth-century) and visited medieval gardens. In the Cocharelli manuscript, members of the Italian nobility stand beside a marble fountain in a walled garden resembling one described by Boccaccio in the *Decameron* (1348), where a group of Florentine aristocrats find sanctuary from the plague:

> The sight of this garden, its form and contrivance … pleased the ladies so much, that they spared not to say, if there was a paradise on earth, it could be in no other form, nor was it possible to add anything to it.

Our own nobility would have conspired on their return to emulate at least some of the elements of Continental gardens in their own walled enclosures (already a feature of fortified towers and courtyard castles), bearing in mind the northern latitude and inhospitable climate of home.

There were other influences at work on the imaginations of deeply devout, high-consuming medieval Scots. Scotland's cultural connection with Flanders had been reinforced after the foundation of Louvain University, where an intellectual elite of Scots clerics and lawyers was educated, as well as by the development of Bruges as a staple port. In the

Ruthven Tapestry: valance from a bed at Balloch (Taymouth Castle) depicts scenes of Adam and Eve in Paradise and their expulsion from the Garden. A true lovers' knot suspended from a ram's head surmounts the Campbell and Ruthven arms of the owners.

Glasgow Museums: Burrell Collection, reproduced by permission.

medieval period new imagery had to be created for remembering the new knowledge in increasingly complex times. The art of memory, devised by Simonides, was passed on and transformed, like every other art – including gardening – from Greece to Rome, to medieval Renaissance Italy, and on to the rest of Europe. As we shall see, James VI was *au fait* with the art of memory, still a potent force in the sixteenth century.

Like so much else, the rosary, a series of devotions dedicated to the Virgin Mary, reached Scotland via the Flemish connection. The Arbuthnot *Book of Hours* (c.1480) shows an image of 'Sancta Maria in sole' surrounded by a five-decade rosary of red beads and pink roses. The *Warburg Hours*, produced in Flanders in the same period, shows Adam and Eve, standing in an orchard. Realistic flowers decorate the border – violets, strawberries (flowering and fruiting, and thus symbolic of the potential of the Christian spirit), borage and daisies.

Precious books of the hours, lavishly illustrated (as in another Flemish example (c.1500) where a gardener and his wife push a huge basket containing a red carnation on a wheelbarrow), were available only to wealthy Scots, and particularly to noblewomen. Like their European counterparts, they would have planted flowers with religious symbolism, thus intensifying their devotion to the cult of the Virgin Mary in their gardens. The white lily (*Lilium candidum*) was symbolic of Mary as the 'beloved' of Solomon and, in early Renaissance paintings, of the Annunciation. Roses, once the sacred flower of Venus, had become associated with Mary; red roses (*Rosa gallica*) signified divine love and the blood of the martyrs, and were grown over trellises and arbours, with hedging of wild roses. Other flowers reflected Christian virtues: the modest violet, humility; the purple iris, the robe of the Virgin; the winged columbine, the dove of the Holy Ghost; carnations, the Incarnation. Most of these flowers appear on the central panel of the magnificent, super-real Portinari altarpiece (1475), commissioned for the Medicis in Bruges, and any Christian visiting a garden of the period would have been able to reinforce his or her faith by 'reading' the flowers. In an age when Scots nobles were both conspicuous *bon viveurs* and pious devotees, the new Christian symbolism translated well to the *hortus conclusus*, as a manifestation of the purity of the Virgin Mary.

The white lily (*Lilium candidum*) (opposite below left) was later associated with the Virgin and symbolised the Annunciation in early Renaissance painting.

'White Lily' from the *Apuleius Platonicus Herbarium*, The Conway Library, Courtauld Institute of Art, reproduced by permission of the Provost and Fellows of Eton College.

Grea crini on uocant·
ad luxum·
Herbe lilu folia tunsa
æ impofita efficacit
fanat· fi humor fue
rit fedat· ad peut
suā serpentis·
herbe lilu bulbū ētito
æi potu dab ipsū etiā
bulbū tritū morsui adpo
ne sanabit· hytimalli spe
cies s̄· vii· quarū alia mafeul
fiue charatias appellatur l'
amigdalo· i copios cometes
pos me routris· alipos· Latini
nos arcos· alia femina fiue mirthi
tis· l'charites· chametis cartris· roma
ni mutilago· tatimallū f̄· baacheut·
capria· alia pa
ralos· fiue tyhi
mallos· peplih
thymallis para
plion· meronton·
Quarta elio fcopos·
denitis tythimallis
latini cicer· colūbinū
ide caphgine·
Quinta qparifias· vīden
tudes· vii platifillos· fiue

cometes· aut
eatacitis ebs co
baheū· Pphe go

Paintings, notably the Flemish Madonna paintings, expressed the symbolic theme of the garden and its flowers. *Annunciation*, a painting by Hans Memling (c.1430–94) in the Burrell Collection, Glasgow, shows the Virgin and her bed, with a botanically accurate lily in a copper pot. A painting in the Capilla Real, Granada, of Virgin and Child (1490) by Memling's follower, Dieric Bouts, shows a Flemish house (reminiscent of late-sixteenth-century Scottish chateaux) with bartizan tower, corbelled roofs and gallery, beyond a garden divided by raised rectangular beds, each four bricks high, sanded paths, *estrades* (trimmed plants trained over tiered hoops) and flowers including lavender, carnations and irises.

Long before the Reformation, Scotland had been an important node on a vast and complex European network, exchanging intellectual and cultural ideas, and demonstrating its awareness of artistic development in the rest of Europe, and, importantly, its imaginative ability to imbue its productions with traditional values of its own. Obviously this applied to gardening too. The fortified house required its herb garden, and why not its formal garden or herber? Garden design had been considered an art form, at least as important as the other arts, certainly since the Italian Renaissance; and Italian garden designs – before the French – had been the catalyst behind the development of gardens further north, in Holland and Germany, Poland, Flanders, England, Ireland and Scotland. As early as the fourteenth century Robert the Bruce supervised the landscaping of his parks and gardens; an elaborate formal garden, the King's Knot, appeared in the Vale of Stirling by 1502. At that time, and long before, the Scottish kings kept menageries – lions' dens and caged animals – in the grounds of their palaces. Menageries were an indispensable feature of the royal holdings that strove to match those of France and Holland. This being the case, they would have cultivated gardens, too, of sufficient merit to impress the many European visitors that came to Scotland, and particularly the ambassadors and knights who came to attend tourneys and great festivals at the palaces of Holyrood, Falkland, Linlithgow and Stirling.

There may have been far more gardens in fifteenth-century Scotland than is commonly supposed. And they would be as lovely and as full of meaning in their own way as any cloister gardens or castle

The Virgin and the
symbolic lily. Hans
Memling (c.1430–94).

Glasgow Museums: Burrell
Collection, reproduced
by permission.

gardens in more remote areas of Europe. Today Poland, for example,
boasts several preserved medieval gardens (fourteenth-century) around
castles and cloisters. Is it not likely that we bowed-headed Scots have
been over-cautious in consigning the traces of ancient terraced gardens

at Linlithgow Palace, Neidpath Castle near Peebles, and the Borders keeps at Hangingshaw, Elibank, Whytebank, Torwoodlee Tower and many others to the *late* sixteenth century? Could the garden ground at Guthrie Castle be much older than supposed? At Guthrie physical remains date from the early 1600s, including the curved garden walls. The family records trace back to the thirteenth century; tradition has it that a Guthrie held the office of Chief Falconer to Malcolm Canmore and records show that in 1468 a later Guthrie, Sir David, Treasurer to James III, obtained a warrant to build a castle with a yett. Some time between that date and 1614, when the garden walls were built at Guthrie Castle, a series of garden terraces had been laid out on the gently sloping, south-facing hill north of the castle. It seems odd, this almost semi-circular garden wall, until you wonder if it was constructed to enclose already existing, earlier terraces, perhaps to protect delicate plants and herbs from high winds and predators: white lilies, roses naturalised and wild, violets, purple irises, columbines, carnations. Essential flowers for an emblematic garden.

Neidpath Castle, Peeblesshire. The terracing is clearly visible on a vignette of Armstrong's Map of Peeblesshire (1775).

Historic Scotland.

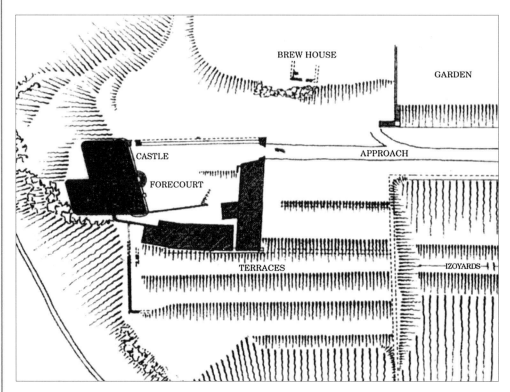

CHAPTER 3

The Pleasaunce at Edzell

BE GUIDED BY NATURE AND DO NOT DEPART FROM IT ...
FOR TRULY ART IS HIDDEN IN NATURE AND HE WHO
CAN DRAW IT OUT POSSESSES IT

Late spring signifies the journey can begin in earnest ... The King's Knot in the Vale of Stirling is the obvious place to start, yet in my imagination I find myself drawn back, again and again, to the incomparable Pleasaunce at Edzell Castle whose embellished walls displayed to me their peerless brio on my first visit last summer. It is as if I must rehearse that visit before I go any further, to prepare the way for the second visit, in full summer, when I shall be half-way through the book.

'It is ane excellent dwelling, a great hous, delicat gardine with walls sumptuously built of hewen stone polisht, with pictures and coats of armes in the walls,' wrote Ochterlony of Guynd, who no doubt 'read' the garden from the windows of the house as was the custom of the time. I, too, have gazed down at the garden's sculpted walls and parterres from the long window of the abandoned Stirling Tower and duly approach the garden gate. Nowadays, Historic Scotland is the keeper of the castle and its enclosed garden, or 'pleasaunce', that was once surrounded by the castle moat. A great deal of the family's history is revealed by the stone-carved Lindsay coat of arms above the gate, inscribed 1604. The knight's helmet indicates that Lord Edzell was knighting champion of Scotland for seven years. The eyepiece, pulled down yet open, indicates that he was titled. Three muzzled bear heads state that the people of his second wife, Dame Isobel Forbes, possessed strength to be reckoned with. The *fez cheque* motif that is repeated again and again on the inside walls reveals Lindsay's membership of the Templar Knights of St John, an honour offered to him in Malta after a crusading journey with Richard III.

Visitors who are fortunate enough to meet the head gardener might wonder if he had jumped down off a Renaissance stage. He certainly seems to be in his element in this enclosed theatrical world where he strives to garden naturally, cutting the box hedges by hand, for example, even if the geometrical grass areas introduced in the twentieth century have to be trimmed by a mechanical mower. And he has made it his business to find out what he can about the extraordinary walls of David Lindsay's Pleasaunce that surround him daily like a Renaissance theatre set.

Before we enter the pleasaunce, the gardener checks

The coat of arms of
David Lindsay of Edzell
and his wife Isobel Forbes
above the Pleasaunce
entrance.

© Sheila Mackay, 2001.

assumptions, such as that we will find bee boles there. No, no, he
insists, bees would have been too irritating to the Lindsay ladies who
graced the gardens. Surely you see my lady go down through the
garden singing? Yes, but she wouldn't have been so inclined to sing with
bees buzzing round her. Birds, yes, the garden was, and still is, a haven
for birds. But bee boles, he says with certainty, would have been
inserted in wall niches in the *outer* courtyard. And he adds that beyond

that courtyard there stretched arable strips for bleaching and drying the linens, for vegetable cultivation and the playing fields referred to by Ochterlony of Guynd in his description of Forfarshire (1678). If you ventured into the woods and parklands in those days you would have found extensive forestation and enclosed parks for deer.

Even if you have heard tell of the fabled walls of the Pleasaunce, they come as a surprise. The first range displays ancient gods and goddesses, or planets as we might call them now. Each of the walls is divided into seven sections with carved, seven-pointed 'mullet' stars, and hewn-out niches repeating the seven pattern, and the *fez cheque* again, this time containers for plants. These always were planting boxes, asserts the gardener, who can tell, he says, by the way they were hollowed out to support earth. The niches are planted with white alyssum and blue lobelia – the Knights Templar black and white check system translated into Saltire blue and white, the Lindsay colours, and the colours of St Andrew.

The planet wall represents Mars, Jupiter, Saturn, Mercury, Venus, the Sun and the Moon in bas-reliefs whose secondary details convey some of the beliefs and interests of the Lindsay family. Luna stands on a fish, tempering the pagan with a symbol of the family's affiliation with Anglicism, my guide suggests. King Saul, a play on 'Sol', holds a flaming torch and a sun on his shield to light his night house. Mars is resplendent in German armour with the initials 'IB' on the halberd. Here was the vital clue that enabled Dr W. Douglas Simpson, then Librarian of Aberdeen University, to trace the stirring provenance of the carvings on the planet wall to the Nuremberg studios of Albrecht Dürer and to publish his findings in the *Proceedings of the Society of Antiquaries of Scotland* (1930–1). Dürer's companion, Georg Pencz, who had signed himself Iörg Bentz (IB), had produced the series of miniature engravings (nos. B.11–17, 1528/9) that are the very source of the sculptures. Years later, Lord Lindsay, on honeymoon with his second wife, saw the engravings and had them recreated on this magnificent East Wall of the garden.

The gardener beckons me into the delightful pavilion at the intersection with the next wall, which complements the bath house (now ruined) that stood at the opposite corner of the garden. Rothiemay's 1647 view of Edinburgh shows a walled parterre garden at

Top.
The wall of the 'Planetary Deities', with its seven divisions, seven-point star nesting boxes and *fez cheque* niches planted with lobelia and alyssum.

Bottom.
Mars, one of the seven 'Planetary Deities' based on an engraving by Georg Pencz from the Dürer Studios at Nuremberg.

3 7

Holyrood Palace with the small building known as Mary's Bath House set in a corner, just like this one. The pavilion offered an escape from the castle, where sweetmeats might be sampled after summer meals and where one could retire to an upstairs bedchamber, these days displaying wooden carvings of the Annunciation, Virgin and Child and the Crucifixion. In summer, in Scotland, garden pavilions offered shelter from downpours. Francis Grose illustrated one at Gowrie House, near Perth, in his *Antiquities of Scotland,* thought to have belonged to the first Earl of Kinnoull who died in 1634. The interior room had a 'coved ceiling, in which are coarsely painted the twelve signs of the Zodiac, the Heathen Gods and Goddesses, and the arms, crest, and cyphers of the Hay family'. (Readers on a serious search for clues might note that Alexander Dicson, who is mentioned later in connection with the Art of Memory at the court of James I and VI, was a member of the Hay family.) On a more practical note, as John Rea the English nursery gardener wrote, the summerhouse should be provided with chairs and a table, not only as a sitting place from which to enjoy the garden but for use when one is digging up and carefully labelling bulbs and setting them there to dry.

The south wall of the Pleasaunce is devoted to the 'liberal arts' considered so important in the Renaissance. Less intricate than the planetary deities, these panels, too, contain delightful details. A mother hen and chick at the feet of Grammatica, for example, might indicate that the learning process is ongoing, passed from one generation to the next, as the gardener suggests. Generous niches stand empty above the wall coping where busts of learned figures of the day might have stood, anticipating the interior feature that became popular in the libraries of grand homes by the neo-classical period. The seven-star holes repeated on this wall were constructed to attract nesting birds and the gardener affirms that robins, wagtails and chaffinches enjoy flitting in and out of them to this day. He runs a sturdy hand over another repeated feature, a stone protuberance in a seven-link pattern, and points out that these carvings were the coping stones of polished stone pilasters that once divided the walls into – of course – the magical number seven. Luna, on the summerhouse, links the east and south walls.

Seven is everywhere. A clue to what? The sacred number of the ancients who adopted it from the seven stars of the Plough, which they

Arithmetica, one of seven bas-reliefs representing the 'liberal arts'.

© Sheila Mackay, 2001.

called the Great Bear? The constellation that was ever-present in the night sky, offering reassurance in the Renaissance world of rapid change?

I wonder.

The third wall continues the *basso continuo* of nesting-box stars, *fez cheques*, pilasters and niches. Here Faith, Hope and Charity, the Christian or Cardinal virtues, romp with Justice, Temperance, Prudence and Fortitude. These charming images are more primitive than the other two groupings and each displays a double spiral which suggests to me the harnessing of the Celtic church to Rome. That is only a hunch, but in the absence of hard facts the Pleasaunce at Edzell invites conjecture.

Emboldened, one might question the ponderous planting of today's garden ground. The sturdy garden walls remained unscathed but the original planting layout disappeared in time. In 1932, the ruins and garden were given over to state care. The garden ground was

Top.
Prudentia, one of seven bas-reliefs representing the 'Christian Virtues'.

Opposite.
The Stirling Tower, Edzell Castle, and the wall of the 'Christian Virtues'.

Both © Sheila Mackay, 2001.

4 I

reconstructed between 1932 and 1938 as a conventional parterre with eight beds, all closed by box hedging, arranged around a sunken central octagonal grass area. The box hedges are given a good clip, by hand shears, once a year. Neatly clipped box knots represent fleurs-de-lys, shamrock, rose and thistle with the Lindsay motto *Dum Spiro Spero*, 'while I breathe I hope'. A large clipped yew stands central, flanked by four roundel yews. In contrast to the delightful dexterity and ingenuity of the carved walls, dripping lobelia, alyssum and French marigolds in season, the garden ground is disappointing. The gardener is hardly in a position to agree, but he does confess that he would prefer a fountain or a sundial to the fusty central yew and, left to his own devices, he would infill the large, hedged shapes of the knots with crushed white sea-shells.

Would David Lindsay – who had no doubt seen Mediterranean and Moorish gardens as well as French and German ones – and who had exerted his imagination to its limits in constructing the walls – really have settled for such banal horticulture? The answer is obviously not and the Renaissance Italian dictum on landscape design (Baccio Bandinelli) springs to mind: 'The things that are built should guide and dominate what is planted.'

But who knows, really, how Sir David Lindsay's garden grew? Certainly the Pleasaunce at Edzell lingers in the memory and teases the imagination.

CHAPTER 4

Royal Gardens in the Landscape

AXIS, PATILLIS, SWEYIS, HOLLIS MATOKIS,

GRAPIS, DEBILLIS AND CUTTING KNIFIS

WITH OTHIR INSTRUMENTIS

The sleeping lion is one of the names Edinburgh folk give to Arthur's Seat. The hill looms or rejoices over Scotland's capital, depending on the weather and the time of year, but it no longer echoes to the roar of the lion and other animals kept in the palace grounds spread below me where, in 1512, Sir John Scharpe was remunerated for work on the 'lioune house'. A lion had been brought from Leith to the Abbey in 1506, an ape was on view in 1535 and in the late sixteenth century Thomas Fenton, keeper of the palace garden, was paid £244 a year 'for keeping, nurisment and intertenement of the kingis grae liounn, tyger and lutervis [lynx] being in his custodie thair'.

Menageries of 'beistis and pettis' – wild and unusual animals from 'divers outlandish lands' – had appeared in Scotland since the early fourteenth century when Robert the Bruce kept a lion. Lions' dens at the palaces of Stirling and Linlithgow suggest the presence of menageries, but most existing references are to Holyrood where a lion yard and lion house were features of the palace grounds from the early sixteenth century. Clearly the Scottish monarchs considered menageries to be an indispensable feature of their style and standards if they were to keep up with countries like France and Holland, which flaunted exotic collections in architectural settings that were the talk of Europe.

The earliest map of the Palace of Holyroodhouse and Arthur's Seat, the so-called English Spy's Map of 1543–4, clearly shows the palace gardens as well as St Anthony's Chapel above St Margaret's Loch. James Gordon of Rothiemay's engraving of Edinburgh (1647) indicates the dykes that delineate the palace gardens not much altered a century later.

Today the chapel is a romantic ruin set on its craggy knoll above St Mary's Loch, a haven for walkers. Up here there is an unrivalled view of Fife and the Firth of Forth in the distance, with the palace and its royal park spread below. The Abbot of Bellenden (1473–1503) is credited with the chapel's construction and was also associated with works at the palace. Holyrood Palace may have remained under monastic control until the sixteenth century since references to lay gardening there only appear in 1504, when Sir John Scharpe was appointed, 'who makis the garding in Edinburgh' by James IV's

Opposite, top.
Royal households kept lions and other wild 'beistis and pettis' from 'divers outlandish lands' in menageries.

From the *Cosmography* of Zakaria al-Kazwini; (Yah. Ms. Ar. 1113), Jewish National and University Library, Jerusalem.

Opposite, below.
The English Spy's Map (1544) is the earliest view of Edinburgh from the north, showing Edinburgh Castle, the Royal Mile, the Palace of Holyroodhouse, Arthur's Seat and the Royal Park.

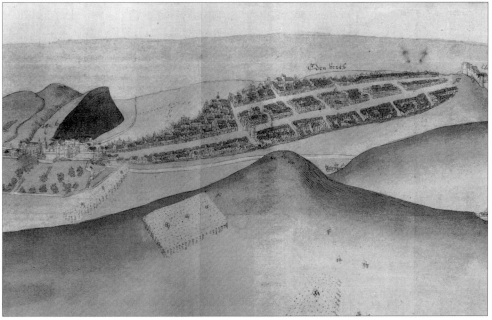

command. Later accounts describe Scharpe as chaplain to the king, and keeper and 'overseer' of the 'gardingis' of Holyrood House as distinct from the gardens of the abbey, and he held these positions until his death in 1538. In 1507 he was paid for 'louch drying' beside the abbey of Holyroodhouse 'for the garding to be maid' and in 1511 payment was made to a carter who 'brocht necessaris to the queens garding'. There had been no queen in Scotland for seventeen years before the 1503 marriage of James IV (1488–1513) to Margaret Tudor, the young daughter of Henry VII of England, which may have spurred on the King to renovate the royal palaces, castles and gardens at Holyrood, Stirling, Linlithgow and Falkland, well before the event. James worked on the main structure of Falkland Palace until his untimely death at Flodden in 1513. To feel the rough stone garden walls at Falkland is to feel the frisson of that past, high enclosing walls ordered by James IV, 'as handsome in complexion and shaped as a man can be', as a visiting Spanish ambassador wrote.

James IV introduced printing to Scotland. In 1507 he set up the first printing press in Scotland under the management of Walter Chepman and Andrew Myllar of Edinburgh. The art of memory survived printing and, chameleon-like, emerged in the occult Hermetic tradition which held that the mind and memory of man become divine through his *magically activated imagination*. It became an occult art, practised by James I and VI (and, almost certainly by earlier Scottish

Paradise depicted as an enclosed garden, 'arbor vitae', with a central mount and planted beds.

From Cosmas Rossellius, *Thesaurus Artificiosae Memoriae*, Venice, 1579.

Opposite.
Alphabet as a memory system includes gardening implements.

From Johannes Romberch, *Congestorium Artificiose Memorie*, ed. of Venice, 1533.

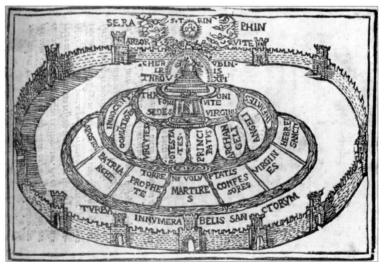

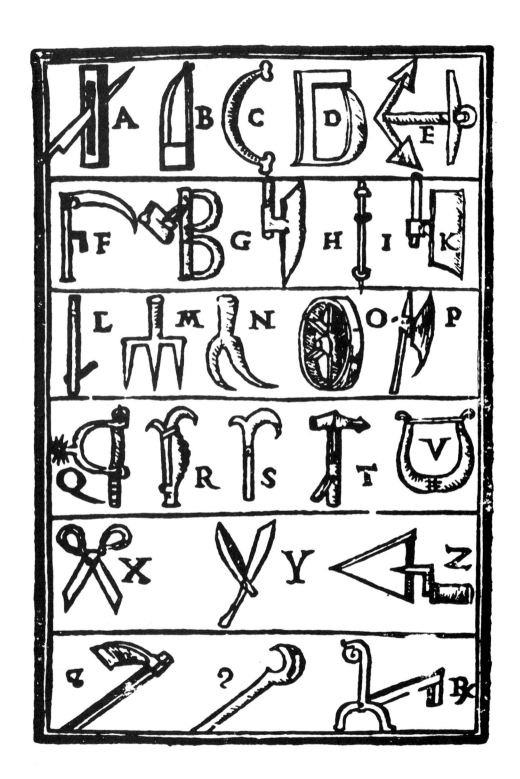

monarchs) and in this form it continued to take a central place in a central European tradition. The *Thamus* of Alexander Dicson 'the Scot', a 'magic art of memory' was published in Leiden in 1597. But the 'talk of Europe', one of the most famous men of the sixteenth century, was the Italian Giulio Camillo Delminio, who invented a compelling Memory Theatre based on the Seven Pillars of Wisdom, symbolic of stable eternity.

Imagination, above all human abilities, was prized during the Renaissance. The Renaissance in Italy had been concerned imaginatively to reconstruct the arts and architecture of Ancient Greece and Rome – and their gardens. The art of memory, one of the most inventive of all the arts, supported the art of rhetoric and performance from Ancient Greece to the Reformation and beyond. Robert Fludd, a practitioner of the art of memory, dedicated his *Ultriusque Cosmi ... Historia* to James I and VI, whose daughter Elizabeth inspired a garden at Heidelberg Castle that was considered the eighth wonder of the world by 1613. Memory and gardens are inseparably linked and the art of memory and the art of gardening merge gloriously in the Pleasaunce of Edzell (1604), where more than anywhere else, our eyes might be opened to hints of the mystery of the Scottish Renaissance and to what we had and what we lost.

Before the invention of printing, artists like Leonardo da Vinci, Albrecht Dürer and Hans Weiditz produced botanically accurate representations of flowers that were 'a world away from most earlier drawings of plants'. Plants provided most of the drugs used in medicine and physicians had to know their flora. But now, printed books, often with decorative woodcuts, superseded the old, laboriously copied herbals and revolutionised the spread of botanical knowledge. Botany as a science – the study of the structure of plants not only for their usefulness in providing cures – began to develop. Doctors, scholars and gardeners throughout Renaissance Europe experimented and communicated on the gripping subject of growing and acclimatising new plants. Herbalists were trained as physicians. The 'father of English botany', William Turner, studied medicine in Italy. His book, *A New Herball* (1551), was a landmark, and like his contemporaries John Gerard (*Herball*, 1597) and John Parkinson (*Paradisi in Sole:*

Paradisus Terrestris, 1629), he was a keen horticulturalist. The study and classification of 'nature' encouraged botanists and physicians to hold a *hortus siccus*, or collection of dried plants. Edinburgh held one by the late seventeenth century when a physic garden, or *hortus medicus*, was established behind the Palace of Holyroodhouse.

There had been designed landscapes at the royal palaces of Falkland, Linlithgow, Stirling, and Holyrood and on aristocratic estates like Hamilton and Kinneil since the thirteenth century. In his retirement Robert the Bruce had involved himself in developing gardens and parkland at Cardross in Dunbartonshire. The monarchy was the least insular layer of society and, with cosmopolitan contacts at the highest level, its members aspired to emulate in style and content contemporary royal landscapes in other parts of Europe. The construction of a great hall (*palatium*) at the castles of both Edinburgh and Stirling marked the climax of medieval monarchy, and the lavish endowment of the Chapel Royal at Stirling in 1501 symbolised the new devout humanism that was to come; *imagination*, above any other quality, distinguished the Renaissance from the medieval world.

The royal palaces were venues for a brilliant Renaissance court imbued with all the arts, and, although gardening was not yet a popular art form, it was regarded as such within the Scottish court. Nobles would have developed within their own estates, courtyard or walled gardens, herb gardens and orchards or *viridariae*. In 1503 James IV ordered lords and lairds to make deer parks, fishponds and doocots on their land to augment the diet of the community. Then as now, garden and estate development was a costly business, prohibitive to all but the most elevated Scots before booming trade in the last quarter of the sixteenth century produced a new elite of merchants and made the emergent middle-class wealthy. It is fairly commonly held that Scotland on the periphery of Europe, Scotland with its terrible climate and terrain, had a low regard for gardens at the time. But Scottish kings, nobles and scholars travelled all over Europe and reinterpreted on their return what they had seen and heard in all the arts – including landscape design. On their return, they had on hand in their cosmopolitan court, whether at Stirling, Edinburgh or Linlithgow, sages who could help them translate new European fashions into a vision that embraced their own native tradition. Like the King, the court

conversed in at least six languages, including French, Italian and Gaelic. Robert Carver, the musician and Augustinian canon of Scone, the poet and Observant Franciscan William of Touris, the poet and churchman William Dunbar, and Sir David Lindsay of the Mount are only a few of the prodigies who illuminated the court of James IV. It is notable that religion, drawn up from the medieval period, influenced music and poetry, and medieval gardens, as we have realised, were places of devotion, templates for their further development in the Renaissance court as 'outdoor rooms' where courtly consultations and entertainments took place and where fashionable figures such the King's Italian alchemist and the King's Gaelic harpist might feel inspired to linger beside scented knots and stroll through flowery grasses. A bonding blend of chivalry and Christianity encouraged the vibrant cult of honour that united James's nobles, who played the 'Knichtly game' of joust and tournament in the royal parks that became increasingly 'designed' as the century progressed.

From the ruined entrance of St Anthony's Chapel the imagination reels, looking down over the former hunting grounds of the royal park where James IV and James V (1513–42) hunted, hawked and shot with the bow and arrow, and Mary, Queen of Scots, held picnic banquets. In 1503 deer were transported here in litters from Falkland. James V sent his own hunting 'retinue' to France in 1536 by ship from Leith. The land below, the gardens, greens and park of Holyrood, the former recreation area of the Stewarts, is a vast empty space in winter that once rang with life.

The Holyrood House records mention a key 'to a stair within the garden for the keeping of the partrikes [partridges] at the kingis command'. Archery butts, real tennis courts and a billiard hall were other diversions enjoyed by the royal household in all their palaces and by nobles on their estates. Three days of feasting at Holyrood followed the Tournament of the Black Knight and Black Lady in the lists at Edinburgh Castle around 1507, whose focus was 'the Tree of Esperance, which grows in the garden of Patience, bearing leaves of Pleasure, the flower of Nobleness, and the fruit of Honour'. Where was this garden of Patience with its Tree of Esperance where each week of the Tournament the five shields of the challengers were hung? Was it

Opposite, top.
The King's Knot, showing the mount in the Vale of Stirling below Stirling Castle.

Photograph courtesy of James Crumley.

Opposite, below.
Box-enclosed knot, Dunbar's Close Garden, Edinburgh.

© Sheila Mackay, 2001.

an allegorical tree? Was the garden of Patience situated at Holyrood? Perhaps we shall never know, but the reference is a reminder that the Renaissance world is difficult for us to enter. There is frustratingly little evidence to tell us what the palace gardens were like, but if sport, chivalry, feasting and the keeping of exotic beasts and pets were so lavishly funded, it is reasonable to assume that the royal gardens, too, attempted to keep up with the standards of the rest of Europe, and particularly France, Holland and Flanders.

From 1502 a New Garden was laid in a corner of the park nearest to Stirling Castle and developed throughout the century. A French gardener worked on the King's Knot at Stirling, sometimes called Scotland's first parterre, in 1530. At the time a parterre was simply an ornate flower bed, usually adjoining the palace or house, but the design of parterres became an art form in the seventeenth century. A less confusing name for the King's Knot might be the King's Mount, since, although the garden of James V is likely to have contained one or more parterres as well as knot pattern layouts, the essential feature is the mount.

Knot designs feature in Roman, Islamic, Celtic and medieval Christian decorative art. Middle Eastern rugs showing knot designs had been imported to Britain at least a century earlier. The *Hypnerotomachia Poliphili* (Venice, 1499) shows the earliest diagrams of garden knots, figures filled with flowers and herbs resembling a 'tapeti' or carpet. (A carpet was called a 'tapies' by Mary of Guise and her daughter Mary, Queen of Scots.) In its simplest form, the knot, a figure of interlacing bands, expressed continuity or even the symbol of infinity. Thomas Hill's book (*The profitable Arte of Gardening*, 1568) shows a 'proper Knotte': 'to be cast in the quarter of a garden, or otherwise as there is sufficient roomth', infilled with thyme or hyssop. The King's Knot was probably in place by 1540 when the new palace was finished for James V and Mary of Guise and contemporary with the mount at Hampton Court. Mary of Guise (1515–60) was a passionate gardener and a major influence in importing French ideas about horticulture and garden design to Scotland. Her first husband had been the Duc de Longueville whose family were well known for introducing exotic plants into France. Sadly, all traces of the plantings and records of the Knot have vanished. It is a skeleton whose layout can

still be 'read' from the palace walls, high above, as a long rectangle with a central square of octagonal turf terraces best seen in winter under a powdering of snow. The central design is the so-called knot, a raised mount with a summerhouse surrounded by a deep moat, offering striking vistas of the castle rock and the Vale of Stirling.

The mount as a feature of post-medieval gardens is thought to be a transmutation of the raised fortification (the motte and bailey castle) with watch tower into raised landscapes within gardens, with fine views and a banqueting or summerhouse, in more peaceful times. The recent reconstruction of St Mary's Pleasance, Haddington, includes a small mount with a view over the pleasance wall of the river that runs through the town. At Hampton Court (1533–4) the ascent to the new mount was by way of paths flanked by stone-carved king's beasts. Visitors reaching the summit, the three-storey Great Round Arbour and Mount Garden, were rewarded with a bird's-eye view of the gardens and the River Thames. Almost a century later when mounts were commonplace in less noble gardens, Francis Bacon wrote (*Of Gardens*, 1625) that an ideal garden should have a mount in the middle formed 'in perfect circles, without any bulwarks or embossments; and the whole mount to be thirty feet high, and some fine banqueting house with some chimneys neatly cast, and without too much glass'. At Atholl in Perthshire, James V, on a hunting expedition, had been put up in 'ane fairie palice of green trymmer wond with birkis' with 'fyne glassin windows in al airttis [parts]'. Like the mount, the 'fairie palice' or summerhouse, and the parterre, the knot developed in the next century as an increasingly complex feature of designed gardens.

The inspiration behind the creation of Renaissance gardens in the rest of Europe at the time originated in the French court, whose symmetrical chateaux were reflected in the intricate geometrical knot-gardens and parterres of their designed landscapes. Taking into account the rugged terrain of Scotland and its inclement weather, was there a distinctive Scottish style of gardening, incorporating traditional approaches to land management as well as knowledge of developments in the rest of Europe? Terracing (uncommon in English and French gardens where ruggedness was not an option) has been noted, at Neidpath Castle, Guthrie Castle, Aberdour Castle, Barncluith House

and the Border keeps, for example, a feature that maximises the use of sloping ground and offers artful views of the surrounding landscape.

The first terraced garden of the Renaissance, the Villa Medici at Fiesole, was the meeting place of Lorenzo de Medici's Platonic Academy, who were 'undoubtedly stimulated by the long terraces and their harmony with the immediate and distant view'. The Italian garden designers harked back to Greece, of course, and to the legendary Terrace Garden of Queen Hatshepsut (c.1500 BC), to the Middle Ages' practice of terracing on the summit of castle walls (for safety's sake) and, in particular, to the thirteenth-century Moorish gardens of the Generalife, Granada, terraced on the slopes above the Alhambra. Terracing offered other options if there was a good water supply. By 1550 the Villa d'Este at Tivoli channelled its abundant water supply into a waterfall and fountain spectacle, unequalled before or since. It requires no great stretch of the imagination to conjure up Scottish travellers, returned from Italy, extolling the Italian terraced gardens and commenting on their suitability, waterfalls, fountains and all, for many Scottish sites. A Slezer engraving gives us a 'distinct hint' of terracing between the palace and the loch at Linlithgow Palace. Is this, asks Neil Hynd, another example of what, in the sixteenth and seventeenth centuries, developed as a particularly Scottish style of garden? At Neidpath Castle near Peebles, one can still trace out a complex terraced garden stepping down to the River Tweed. References exist to gardening at Neidpath Castle in 1581. Four minor castles in Selkirkshire – Hangingshaw, Elibank, Whytebank and Torwoodlee Tower – had terraced gardens at least by the late sixteenth century, and probably earlier. The garden of Barncluith House, Lanarkshire, has a steeply sloping south-facing terrace garden laid out in the same period, with linking steps, topiary and a banqueting house.

The 4th Earl of Morton, Chancellor in Mary's reign, and Regent from 1572, lived in opulent style at Aberdour Castle, where there was an elaborately terraced garden to the south of the building. After Morton was forced out of office in 1578 he went to live with his cousin at Loch Leven Castle where 'he busied himself in making walls and alleys, in drawing of garden plots', according to the *Account of the Douglasses*. Surely these were *designs* of walls, alleys and garden plots for Morton's own Aberdour Castle, rather than actual earthwork schemes at the 'water-girt' Loch Leven? A drawing exists showing the Aberdour terracing and the garden as might have been – an imagined landscape for the Earl of Morton, by John Knight in the 1980s. The Earl exemplifies the fate of many Scottish nobles who swung into and out of royal favour, and in fallow times retreated to their country estates where they turned their cultured minds to improving their lands and gardens.

During the reign of James V the widespread European vogue for planting formal gardens, rather than simply using garden ground for sport and recreation, had been spurred on by the many Scots travelling back and forth to the Continent as ambassadors and scholars. They must also have brought back samples of seeds, plants, trees, shrubs and bulbs and descriptions of foreign gardens and of triumphal court festivals performed in the designed landscapes surrounding palaces and castles. These dazzling displays, like the Tournament of the Black Knight and Black Lady at Edinburgh Castle, were intended to impress foreign visitors with the wealth and power of the court that hosted them. Scotland was relatively poor at the time; nevertheless it put its best knights forward. Catherine de Medici used the festivals to bring together opposing religious parties during a period of relative peace in France. Contemporary printed accounts of the Bayonne festival of

'Wild Heilanmen' like the ones here in the army of Gustavus Adolphus of Sweden, at Stettin in 1630, were popular figures at European festivals and tourneys.

'Wild Heilanman' from the Archives of the School of Scottish Studies, ref: DII a 6360, reproduced by permission.

1565 describe a dazzling musical water-spectacle featuring Sirens singing songs of peace as the climax to a series of other entertainments including a 'course' in which participants wore costumes of many nations and 'Wild Scotsmen' were popular; a tournament between 'Knights of Great Britain and Ireland' during which cartels were recited to music and two chariots representing 'Virtue and Love' carried ladies symbolising heroic Virtue, Prudence, Valiance, Justice and Temperance; an attack and defence of a magical castle; a rescue of enchanted knights and ladies turned into rocks.

Pre-Reformation Scotland's most vital ally was France, its church tied to Rome. However, the kingdom was also an important node on the wider network that traded cultural and traditional ideas and practices, as well as goods and people, which spread by way of the North Sea, not only to France and the Low Countries, Italy and England but also north to the Baltic. Taking a lead from the court, like all the other arts, the sources for garden design and content must have been cosmopolitan, and certainly considerably Dutch and Flemish, given Scotland's vigorous trade with these countries. However, what records exist of designed landscapes for the first half of the century indicate a dominant French influence furthered by Mary of Guise.

French gardens had been influenced by Islamic and Italian gardens since the twelfth century. By the sixteenth century gardens in France had been incorporated into the overall design of chateaux according to Vitruvian ideals of beauty as harmony of all aspects, in this case, of the landscape. There was a shift of focus from horticulture to architecture. Axial approaches, courtyard reception area and drainage canals featured in landscape designs, and gardens, contained within a rectangular plan, included parterres, garden sculpture, pavilions and *bosquets* (small wooded areas). By the middle of the century, French formal gardens often displayed elaborate artifices, such as grottoes, and the first printed designs for parterres in geometrical patterns appeared in a book of 1537, though actual parterres had appeared in gardens well before that. The availability of pattern books must have assisted Scots to create and develop parterre designs in their own grounds. Rothiemay's 1647 'Bird's Eye View' map shows elaborate parterres in the palace gardens at Holyrood, and although the map was produced in the next century, many of its features – including the

Heat-retaining walls with bee skeps in the boles at Kellie Castle.

© Brinsley Burbridge, Royal Botanic Garden, Edinburgh.

56

layout of the palace gardens (is the queen's garding and the Garden of Patience here?) and the long gardens behind the houses of the Canongate – may well have been in place during the reign of James V or even earlier.

Although the idea would not be actualised in France until the next century – in the designed landscape at Vaux-le-Vicomte (1656–61), and in Scotland, on a modest, but still impressive scale at Sir William Bruce's Balcaskie and Kinross House – French architectural drawings showed the desirability of opening out beyond the enclosed world of the Renaissance by developing a wide flat area, framed by trees, to display the chateau to its best advantage.

The sixteenth-century thanes of Cawdor might well have visited Pluscarden Abbey at the time of Lubias's tenure, and may even have adopted elements of his approach to their own designed landscape where the Lower Garden or Kitchen Garden was cut into a bank whose retaining stone walls are medieval. Gardens existed at Cawdor Castle, but their first recorded mention, including an orchard, is dated 1635. At Pluscarden, there is very little left of Lubias's design, yet I am not disappointed to have come here in spring, to have approached the abbey by way of its wide hill-enclosed valley, to have experienced the timeless spirit of the place.

The first person I meet is a monk whizzing over a side lawn of the abbey grounds on a motorised mower, his Benedictine brown habit carefully tucked up, and I remember a private visit to secular Ardchattan some years ago, whose secular owner relished the same motorised method of trimming his lawn. Later we sat in his living room with its Romanesque arch and pillars enjoying a glass of claret. At Ardchattan Priory I could appreciate the overlays of architecture that feature in so many of Scotland's buildings. Ardchattan, Beauly and Pluscarden, three thirteenth-century monastic foundations, their gardens mostly missing.

The Pluscarden monk gets off his machine and leads me to the walled garden. On the way, I see the Irish yews planted where two paths meet, old box hedging growing near the remains of an acacia tree and other tree specimens including holm oak, copper beech, lime, cypress and two ancient yews, all thought to date back to the Frenchman

Lubias's landscape design. In the walled garden another monk is preparing the fertile soil for soft fruits and vegetables. This area has been the abbey's market garden for four centuries, and any French-style knot garden or orchards, if they existed, have long since gone. Nowadays this market garden is the private domain of the Benedictine order. There are golden bee boles set in alcoves on the north wall, though, like honeyed icons of that earlier age. Inset beehives were part of Lubias's design for the north wall. Once their nestling straw skeps produced candlewax for divine service. These days they supply the monastic community with wild honey.

It was far from unusual to find French gardeners like Guillaume Lubias and other craftsmen at work in sixteenth-century Scotland. There is mention of a French gardener at Holyrood in 1536 and Scottish gardeners, like one from Aberdour Castle, were already travelling to France and other European countries to work. Later, Scots gardeners were employed in the laying out of the gardens at the Palace of Versailles. It was a two-way traffic. Even as Guillaume Lubias directed the design of the Morayshire garden, the young James V was engaged in extensive works on the Renaissance palaces at Falkland and Stirling Castle. ('Awa' tae Freuchie whaur the Froggies bide', a phrase still heard locally, is said to have originated when French workers lived at the village of Freuchie near Falkland.) The involvement of French gardeners at a senior level, and the presence of French religious orders in Scotland who themselves engaged French designers such as Lubias to work on their abbey gardens, must have influenced immeasurably the design and content of royal and aristocratic gardens. A French gardener, thought to be Bertrand Gallotre, was created 'principall gardinar of oure soverane lordis zardis [yards] and gardingis for all the dais of his life' at Stirling in 1536 and may have supervised a Mr Robert Moneypenny at Holyrood. The King enclosed the royal park at Holyrood around 1541 with stones quarried from Salisbury Crags and had already spent considerable sums on improving Holyrood House and creating a new garden for Madeleine de Valois, his first consort.

Mary, Queen of Scots (1561–7), fresh from France and imbued with a love of gardens as places of entertainment through her knowledge of its court, and in particular of Catherine de Medici, stayed at Falkland every year from 1561 to 1565. Here she loved to play

as a country girl in its parks and woods, riding out 'like Diana, goddess
of the chase, to fly her falcons or hunt in the forest, her brilliant court
following in a colourful calvacade' or strolling in the garden with her
'four Maries', Fleming, Bethune, Livingstone and Seton. Surely she
knew the oral history of this wonderful place, so filled with the
influence of France where she had grown up?

Records of the garden and gardeners' wages existed a century
earlier. In 1485 over eight barrels of onions had been produced at
Falkland and three years later the garden was enclosed with a fence and
an existing wide lawn extended to make 'the lang butts' required in the
practice of archery. Mary of Guelders laid out a walk near the drive
between two oaks known as the 'Queen's Quarrels', planted, perhaps,
to provide wood for the quarrels, or arrows, for the cross-bow.

The Holyrood House accounts offer an intriguing list of the
tools required by gardeners of the time. Robert Moneypenny was paid
for an evocative range of garden tools in 1538 including 'axis', 'sweyis',
'hollis matokis', 'grapis', 'debillis' and 'cutting knifis with othir instrumentis' (axes, saws, matchets, pronged forks, dibbers, knives and other
instruments). And what did Renaissance gardeners wear? In 1542, hose
and a doublet as well as 'ane goun, 5 elnis half elne Frenche blak' were
delivered to 'John Ouchter, gardener in Holyrudhouse'. Perhaps Mr
Ouchter wore the French black gown while working in the garden, the
hose and doublet on courtly occasions out of doors? With such an
elaborate kit and range of gardening tools, serious gardening must have
gone on at Holyrood. Mary, Queen of Scots, is said to have constantly
received ambassadors and statesmen out of doors. It is unthinkable that
the garden would have been other than delightful.

CHAPTER 5

'Gentimenis Places and Gret Palices'

THAIR WAS THE GOD OF GARDENS *Priapus*,

THAIR WAS THE GOD OF WILDERNESS *Phanus*,

AND *Janus* GOD OF ENTRIES DELECTABLE

Warmer weather raises a thick haar from the Forth. Arthur's Seat has disappeared under a silver-grey blanket, swirled about by a frisky wind. Mist here, as in the Highlands, evokes romantic notions of the past and encourages me to conjure up Mary, Queen of Scots, picnicking here as she liked to at Falkland. The keeper of the Holyroodhouse park in 1566–7 was Johnne Huntar, Burgess of the Canongate, and I wonder whether Hunter's Bog, that wide high valley above the palace, was named after him. One of his tasks was to plant and sow broom at the Queen's expense and to keep and brand her sheep.

For several years there has been no water in the valley, but the past two or three wet summers, added to Historic Scotland's recent decision to block off drainage channels in order to create a wetland of Hunter's Bog, have resulted in a lochan where rushes have been quick to spring up and toads to breed. On summer nights, the tiny creatures abound in the twilight, recalling to me their representation on a cushion cover embroidered by the Queen's own hand. Records indicate that for at least one of Mary's picnics the lochan had been dammed up to create an even greater spread of water and it is possible that the result was a loch large enough to contain a water spectacle.

In early summer the gorse splashes like sunshine on the slopes of Arthur's Seat and smells of coconut. On such a day, on 17 May 1562 to be precise, the 5th Lord Fleming married Elizabeth Ross, heiress of Ross and Halkett. Mary, who loved spectacle, provided a banquet at the end of Hunter's Bog Loch. In addition to the Queen, many Scottish nobles and the ambassadors of England and Sweden were present. Looking down on Hunter's Bog I struggle to recreate the Ross-Fleming wedding party in my imagination complete with a water-spectacle, albeit modest in comparison with a French festival such as the one Catherine de Medici put on at Bayonne in 1565. Mary and Catherine corresponded and the fun-loving, culturally astute Mary is almost certain to have made the event an adventure, emulating elements of the Valois festivals. At Bayonne, at midsummer, the French royal party crossed in a barge to an island, attacking an artificial whale as they sailed. Neptune floated by in a chariot drawn by seahorses and addressed the occupants of the barge in verses recited to music supplied by Tritons. Arion sang on a dolphin accompanied by violinists concealed on the shore. Three

Sirens sang and when the party landed, shepherds and shepherdesses danced to the music of bagpipes before the party walked to a banqueting hall in the wood where nine nymphs danced a ballet.

It is not difficult to imagine an entertainment on a smaller scale here, at Hunter's Bog, wooded in those days when it was a feature of the enclosed royal hunting park: the water, the barge crossing, the artificial sea-creatures, the musicians and costumed dancers, the banqueting hall. Certainly, with sophisticated ambassadors present, Mary would have been anxious to demonstrate Scotland keeping up with the rest of Europe, and would have spared no effort or expense for the wedding banquet.

Walking along the track that circumvents Hunter's Bog lochan, I wonder if I have detoured too far from garden paths, then I think not. The Renaissance festivals indicate the increasing use of the designed landscape for recreation and spectacle, and, vitally, as outside theatres for the rehearsal of themes important to the era all over Europe. I reflect, too, that if large sums of money were spent on costuming these events, on constructing what were essentially outdoors stage-flats and theatrical props, and on accommodating the foreign and local visitors that flocked to them, no expense would have been spared on gardens. Indeed, the gardens, and particularly the courtyard or parterre garden, would have served as foyers to esplanade or parkland, foregathering areas before the main spectacle, and in the spirit of the times, even in Scotland, the gardens would have been lush and perfumed. They became known as 'pleasaunces'.

Theatre provided spectacle. The court poet, David Lindsay's, *Ane Satyre of the Three Estaitis*, had been performed for the court at Linlithgow in 1540, at Cupar, Fife, in 1552 and in front of the Queen Regent and a large audience on the lower slopes of Calton Hill in Edinburgh. Given our temperamental climate, it is unlikely that theatrical performances would have been held out of doors with no protection from wind and rain. Semi-permanent constructions, timber theatres probably existed in Scotland, and like their English and European counterparts, some must have been set in gardens, like the garden imagined for George Jamesone, the Scots 'pictor' later in the book.

Poems written before 1600 praise gardens well stocked with 'Herb and Flowir, and tender Plants most sweet, and grene Leivs' and, not

uncommonly, lines evoke the garden as a place of erotic encounter where 'to Venus, Love's bonny Queen, they sang Ballads of Love on Harp and Lute, with amorous notes most lustily devised'. The God of Gardens was Priapus, who encouraged 'mony a lusty Kiss', and William Dunbar's *The Goldin Targe* imagines the lover's tender body lying beside his beloved's – 'So proper set, quhilk Nature has provyde With every Plesour, that thou mayst divyne'. Here is Dunbar's tribute to the allegorical style of the *Roman de la Rose* and its theme of courtly love; the poem was 'particularly quotted by Sir David Lindsay [of The Mount]', according to Allan Ramsay who published the poem in *The Evergreen: Being a Collection of Scots Poems Wrote by the Ingenious before 1600* (1724).

Dunbar describes an entertainment with music and water-spectacle held in a garden:

> Thair was the God of Gardens *Priapus*,
> Thair was the God of Wilderness *Phanus*,
>   And *Janus* God of Entries delectable.
> Thair was the God of Oceans *Neptunus*:
> Thair was the God of Winds bauld *Eolus*,
>   With variant Blasts lyke to an Lord unstable,
> Thair was blyth *Bachus* glader of the Table
> Thair *Pluto* was, that elritch Incubus,
>   In Cloke of Grene, his Court was clade in Sable.

Particularly in Scotland, it was vital to make use of summer – 'For every Thing but for a Season is' – from 'lusty May' onwards when the birds sing 'Amang the tendir Odours reid and quhyt [red and white], Quhois Harmony to heir was grit Delyt' since 'The Rose, the Lilly, and the Violet, Unpult, sone wither.'

By the middle of the century, introduced bulbs, tubers and other plants (originally wild species from Asia) combined with introductions from the New World to revolutionise gardening style and potential in Renaissance Europe. The incredible discoveries of Busbecq, the cultured Flemish ambassador to the Ottoman Sultan in Constantinople from 1554, must have reached the ears of northern horticulturalists, including Scots, well before the deluge of flora he discovered arrived in our ports. Here was a feast for the imagination, a real-life scene from a fantastical work like *Tales from the Arabian Nights*. Travelling the road from Adrianople in winter, the astonished Ambassador Busbecq came across dazzling displays of narcissi, hyacinths and tulips in wild places and later paid a considerable sum for bulbs and seeds to send to the north. Busbecq also introduced the lilac and the horse chestnut. Many of the specimens were sent to the legendary Flemish doctor and botanist, Charles de l'Ecluse or Carlos Clusius, at the imperial court in Vienna, who corresponded with English botanists. Within a hundred years of the establishment of political contacts with the Ottoman Empire, twenty times the number of plants than in the preceding two thousand years entered Europe.

Scots must have been astonished to see the first imported onion-like bulbs and tubers produce riotously coloured, shaped and scented flowers: tulips, narcissi, lilies, irises, hyacinths. To begin with these horticultural incomers were available only to a specialist elite – to physicians, botanists, nobles and wealthy merchants – among whom secular plant collecting became all the rage. Some specimens came from the Far East. There was a 'plant route' (rather like the 'Silk Route') that ran from the Far East to the Middle East to Italy and had tributaries too, from Spain to Italy and France, from Italy to France, from South America to Portugal and Spain; and, last, from all the world in a deluge to Holland and to England – and from the entrepots of the Low Countries to the Scottish ports.

The floral deluge energised the study of medicine and fed the development of botany as a science. The 1545 Botanical Gardens at Padua were followed by others at Pisa, Leiden, Leipzig, Montpellier, Strasbourg, Paris and, by 1632, Oxford. Before 1700 Britain had three botanical gardens at Oxford, Edinburgh (1670) and Chelsea (1673). In 1587 the Dutch horticulturalists, who had recognised the importance of the scientific study of plants, set up the Hortus Botanicus Academicus Lugduni-Batavorum whose second director, Doctor Clusius, introduced and successfully cultivated many tulips, irises, crocuses and bulbous plants in the early seventeenth century. By 1592, Doctor Clusius had created a *hortus botanicus* rather than a *hortus medicus* at Leiden. After that, slowly but surely, physic gardens evolved into botanical gardens, as happened in Edinburgh a century later.

Among the elite, the use of gardens as outdoor rooms for entertainment throughout the century echoed the Renaissance taste for a more open humanism in reaction to the enclosed medieval world, symbolised by the *hortus conclusus*. The gardens of the counts of Holland at The Hague had been laid out by 1460 as a series of outdoor rooms closely integrated with the castle, containing 'flowery medes', turf seats, arbours, trellised roses, lavender and carnations, and an ornate pavilion crowned with gilded statues of the counts. Netherlandish garden design (closely and importantly linked with that of the House of Burgundy) exerted a strong influence on the development of gardens in northern Europe during the Renaissance and after the Reformation. The great Renaissance humanist, Desiderius Erasmus, evoked an ideal and emblematic garden in *The Godly Feast* (1522). Hector Boece, first principal of Aberdeen University and author of *Scotorum Historiae*, was a close friend of Erasmus. James IV sent his illegitimate sons, Alexander (later Archbishop of St Andrews) and James, to Italy to be tutored by Erasmus. Boece and the royal pupils were only one fine link of an intricately woven European network that absorbed standard Erasmian components as applied to gardens, such as galleries, trompe-l'œil ornament, fountains and parterres for rare plants cultivated by renowned Dutch horticulturalists. Erasmian features were later incorporated into the Dutch Mannerist garden designs of Hans Vredeman de Vries (1527–c.1606), a painter, decorator and engineer whose crucial contribution was to regard garden design as an art form. In the next century, Inigo Jones and De Caus in London and George Jamesone in Scotland followed in his footsteps. Through de Vries's work abroad and through the dissemination of his engraved garden designs (*Hortorum viridariorumque …*, Antwerp, 1583), his Mannerist gardens were highly regarded well beyond the borders of the Netherlands, and must have been one of the influences on the development of the Pleasaunce at Edzell.

A delightful account finds Mary, Queen of Scots, in the garden at Edzell half a century earlier. Three months after the Ross-Fleming wedding, in August, 1562, Mary spent the night at Edzell on her famous tour of the north. The visit is described, albeit three centuries later, by Lord Lindsay, drawing on his family's oral history and written records in *The Lives of the Lindsays*.

Masked Venetian figures from the *Album Amicorum* of Sir Michael Balfour, c.1596, hint at the Europolitan consciousness of late sixteenth-century Scots.

Reproduced by permission of the National Library of Scotland.

Imagination can easily picture the still young and blooming Countess [Lindsay] and her fair train of sons and daughters, receiving her [Queen Mary] at the great gates of the Castle. The Queen held a council that day at Edzell – in all probability it took place in the pleasance or garden, according to her constant habit of receiving ambassadors and discussing affairs of state with her ministers and nobles, out of doors.

Looking west from the front elevation of Edzell Castle, Mary would have seen the mound in the Strathmore valley where the original motte castle of Edzell had been built. The Crawford Lindsays acquired the estate in 1358 but towards the end of the fifteenth century the family required a new home and removed into a new towerhouse built on the site of the present castle. This building was considerably expanded with the addition of a gatehouse range, added to the tower around 1553, five years before David of Edzell, 9th Earl of Crawford, died, leaving the Countess, Catherine Campbell, in charge.

The Lives of the Lindsays offers fascinating glimpses of family life at Edzell. Catherine's son David (b.1551) and his brother were 'brought up at Edzell among their clansmen, and on reaching the fit age were sent to pursue their studies on the Continent under the care of Mr James Larson, afterwards the well-known colleague of John Knox'. They studied at Paris and travelled there via Dieppe where they were looked after by a Scottish merchant. It was this David, the 10th Earl of Crawford, who would transform the pleasant garden into a work of art by 1604.

The population of Scotland increased by something like 50 per cent between 1500 and 1650. Poverty affected every layer of society, rural and urban, Highland and Lowland. But within that time span, sometimes referred to by social historians as the 'lang sixteenth century', there were pockets of expansion when money was to be made and when new professions offered opportunities, including landscape gardening, to a 'middling sort'. In garden history terms, there was a short sixteenth century, after 1570 when homes for the newly affluent sprang up in the Highlands and the Lowlands, in cities and towns, all with garden ground. A second, even greater homes-and-gardens boom followed the 1707 Union.

Designed landscapes, other than royal, noble or monastic, came late to the north. Until the middle of the sixteenth century most landowners had been too preoccupied with survival to contemplate putting aside the sword in favour of the spade. They would have grown vegetables, of course, and herbs for culinary and medicinal purposes in walled garden extensions to the old fortified castles of the local laird or clan chief. Religious and political wrangling rumbled on in the background. Reformation, that political and religious revolution against the Roman Catholic Church and the threat of rule from France, swept away sculptures and clerestory windows, and, probably, the 'idolatrous' gardens of the unconverted. But for many the world had become relatively settled. More peaceful times encouraged interest in landscape and nature and booming trade provided the cash for merchants to develop their homes and gardens.

Some were slow to leave their great stone medieval shells. The Countess of Angus remained, tortoise-like, in the noble Bothwell Castle, the Earl of Argyll held to Dunstaffnage and Skipness, so did the Earl of Atholl to Balvenie, while lesser lairds constructed towerhouse gems like Claypotts, Carsluith, Tolquhon and Aboyne, and merchants developed 'places' and 'palices', townhouses and tenements. The Renaissance world no longer required the fortified castle-broch blueprint, but the basic form translated well to the new domestic towerhouse and its offspring tenements. Individual variations, of L-, Z-, T- or E-plans were developed from simple rectangles according to the requirements of the owner or family. Harled stone towers, pitched roofs (sometimes carried on barrel vaults) with 'corbie' or 'crowstep' gables, crenellated and corbelled parapets, angled turrets or 'bartizans' (borrowed from the French) celebrated the owner's wealth. These buildings were Scotland's first ideal homes, attuned to landscape and climate, in which the vertical, fortified forms of the ancestors lingered on, signalling aspiration to power, wealth, status and, not least, to divine approbation.

The Heracletian maxim 'As Above, So Below' expressed the consciousness of the sixteenth and seventeenth centuries and accounts for the adoption of celestial imagery in decorative painting. The hierarchy of the household, with the noble or laird at its head, was seen as a reflection of the *macrocosm* with God at its head and centre. Similarly, the hierarchy of society, with the monarch at its head, was

God-given, and based on the idea of a natural world ruled over by God, in which man was but a *microcosm* of the universe, his animal passions subject to his will. An activated imagination linked the two.

Every building displayed common components as well as unique vernacular features. The same would be true of the gardens. The financial and administrative aspects of constructing a building were dealt with by masters of works, and master masons and master wrights were probably responsible for the design. The king had his architects, but professional architects for less elevated clients only emerged in the late seventeenth century. The team that constructed a building probably also laid out the garden.

Scotland was a predominantly rural nation, with marked differences in prosperity, landscape and even climate between one area and another. Bishop Leslie marvelled at the 'orchardes, and fruitful gairdings' of Morayshire in 1578, where fertile land and high agricultural returns encouraged the creation of Renaissance houses including Boyne and Cullen. Their owners judged the world beyond their walls to be safe enough to allow the garden to expand and develop for 'delight's sake'. The gardens of the nobility became increasingly sophisticated.

'Gentimenis places and gret palices ma sal ye find in na place than in Fife', Bishop Leslie remarked, and James VI (1567–1625) on inheriting that kingdom is said to have likened Fife to a tattered cloak fringed with gold. There were fortunes to be made from coal mining and salt manufacture all along the coast. In St Andrews, for centuries the most important pilgrimage site in Europe after Santiago de Compostela, long rigs behind the houses of wealthy merchants incorporated paved courts, perfume gardens, promenading gardens, orchards, shaped lawns and dazzling paths of crushed sea-shells in 1538; loggias and Erasmian galleries extended out into the gardens as viewing places for the creations below, according to a reconstruction print by Jurek Pütter (1991) which draws on Netherlandish Renaissance gardens. Sir George Bruce of Culross Palace was one of many entrepreneurial merchants who seized the fruits of commerce so that by 1611 he looked south over the Firth of Forth through the half-lead-glazed windows with half-shutters of his fine mansion, and north over his high terraced gardens.

CHAPTER 6

'A Delictible Time of Peax'

'THE FORE-HOWSIS OF THE STREITS ... WAR ALL
HUNG WITH MAGNIFIK TAPESTRIE, WITH PAYNTIT
HISTOREIS, AND WITH THE EFFEGEIS OF
NOBLE MEN AND WEMEN'

To a gardening member of the 'middling sort' in Renaissance Scotland, a garden might be part of a 'land' or a 'rig', the garden itself might be a 'pleasaunce', '*hortus*', 'gardyn', 'garding' or a '*vidriarium*', especially if it had an orchard. The garden, usually hedged in or walled in, was the most intensively used and managed area of the landscape surrounding the house, and had an intimate relationship with the house itself. 'Landscape' refers to the wider area of ground in which the garden is situated, usually with woods and shelterbelts. Garden walls were of rubble masonry which reflected the colours of the surrounding soil and landscape; the walls of Fife that tend towards gold change subtly but surely as you drive north towards Edzell with its sandstone walls of Indian red veined with white, a subtly different red from the walls of East Lothian, where rich brownish-red soil produces succulent berries and Kerr's Pink potatoes.

An Englishman, Thomas Tusser, published his *Hundred Good Points of Husbandry* in 1557 and enlarged the work in 1573 when it appeared as *Five Hundred Points of Good Husbandry*. It was a book for the small gardener – and his wife – and its down-to-earth wisdom delivered in rhymed couplets made it extremely popular. This was garden as craft. Twelve editions were recorded in Elizabeth's reign. Tusser's book, one of several books about small gardens and gardening to appear in England from the middle of the century, must have fallen into Scottish hands. In Scotland the small garden was developing too. Tusser's book is believed to have influenced the first Scottish gardening book: John Reid's *The Scots Gard'ner* (1683). Other books such as John Gerard's *Herbal* (1597) and William Turnbull's *New Herball* (1551) are testimony to the growing interest in gardens among ordinary folk. The orchard and fruit trees were the man's province. Flowers, culinary plants and herbs were tended by women:

> In March and in April, from morning to night,
> In sowing and setting, good housewives delight;
> To have in a garden, or other like plot,
> To trim up their house, and to furnish their pot.

In the 'model garden' in January, peas and beans were set, raspberries and roses and other fruit trees and shrubs were planted. In February

The first Scottish gardening book, John Reid's *The Scots Gard'ner*, was published in 1683.

THE
SCOTS GARD'NER

IN TWO PARTS,

The First of Contriving and Planting
GARDENS, ORCHARDS, AVENUES, GROVES:
With new and profitable wayes of Levelling; and how to
Meafure and Divide Land.

The Second of the Propagation & Improvement of
FORREST, and FRUIT-TREES, KITCHEN-
HEARBES, ROOTS and FRUITS:
With fome *Phyfick Hearbs*, *Shrubs* and *Flowers*.

Appendix fhewing how to ufe the Fruits of the Garden:
Whereunto is annexed

The GARD'NERS KALENDAR.

Publifhed for the Climate of SCOTLAND

By JOHN REID Gard'ner.

Edinburgh, Printed by DAVID LINDSAY, and his
Partners, at the foot of *Heriot's* Bridge, 1683.

rouncival peas were staked. Seeds and herbs were planted in March and April; 43 herbs were listed, including gromwell, saxifrage and mandrake, with marigolds, primrose and violets, the 'blessed thistle' (*Carduus benedictus*), the sea holly (*Eryngium*) and bay (*Laurus nobilis*). Later in the year came the picking:

> The gooseberry, respis, and roses all three
> With strawberries under them trimly agree.

This suggests that plants were mingled and the popular wild strawberry (*Fragaria vesca*) collected from the countryside. In Scotland, a group of French gardeners, the Fraisiers (later, Frasers), were famed for their strawberry cultivation and incorporated three strawberries into the clan crest:

> Wife into the garden, and set me a plot,
> Of strawberry roots, of the best to be got:
> Such growing abroad, among thorns in the wood,
> Well chosen and picked, prove excellent good.

In an expansive age the enclosing walls were high and protective against rain and wind as well as rabbits, deer and other gnawing predators. 'The gardens', formal or kitchen, sprang from the same source and often overlapped, thus embracing within their walls both the oldest and the most recent examples of designs and technique. You may come across a walled kitchen garden originally planted as a formal garden, for example. At Cawdor the lower walled garden has developed through several cycles, from a formal mixed vegetable garden to a kitchen garden and now back to a formal garden with the planting of a new maze and a knot garden. However small their own patch, the new-style gardeners must have emulated gardens on grand estates. De Witt's painting, *Village Dance at Lowland Wedding* (Royal Scottish Museum), vividly conveys the importance of music and dancing in the lives of ordinary folk, who supplied the large numbers of hands-on gardener-horticulturalists already emigrating over the Border to find work on English estates. Many of the gardens left unattended reverted to wilderness and rubble and became our lost gardens. Sometimes

A panel from the Traquair House embroideries in sampler or emblem-book style depicts fruiting plants including pomegranate, pear, grape and strawberry as well as exotic birds and beasts.

© The Royal Commission on the Ancient and Historical Monuments of Scotland.

landowners of more than one estate rented out and lived elsewhere. While the 5th Earl of Haddington lived on his wife's estate at Rothes, the tenanted policies at Tyninghame deteriorated badly, with 'hedges uprooted, mounds and banks ploughed level'.

A garden may begin at any point along the outline of a building where it meets the ground, and where there is convenient ground human beings have an instinct to grow things. Although Scotland was poor at the time, it is impossible not to imagine its people encouraging wild flowers and escapees from the gardens of the rich to flourish in their patch, however humble, along with vegetables and vital herbs grown for the kitchen and for medicinal purposes. Wherever there was a dwelling of any kind, be it a black house or a cottage tied to the castle of a feudal lord, Scots would have planted whatever they could get their hands on that would grow. After all, these people were the close forebears of the top-class Scottish gardeners that would soon be in demand, on a large scale, in England and Europe.

Little is known of the housing of the rural poor, though the visitor John Ray described 'pitiful cots, built of stone, and covered with turves, having in them but one room, many of them no chimneys, the windows very small holes and not glazed' in East Lothian. Vernacular cots varied from place to place, but remained 'pitiful' through the eighteenth century. What little joy there was in life may have included the scent of wild honeysuckle and roses in summer and wayside berries for the eating in autumn. Deborah Howard describes their 'virtually biodegradable housing, made of rubble stonework and roofed with turf …. Only the roof timbers were valuable, and these could be removed and reused whenever the family was forced to move.' The urban and rural poor lived wretched lives, starkly so in contrast to the fortunes that merchants and landowners were making in the last decades of the century.

After a long slump, export trade took an upturn around 1570 and, twenty years later, many merchants and landowners found themselves with fortunes. A French visitor, the Duc de Rohan, claimed in 1600 to have counted over a hundred chateaux set in the countryside, from the walls of Edinburgh Castle. Michael Lynch suggests two symbols of the period:

Gladstone's Land, a six-storey, luxury flatted tenement built c.1600 in Edinburgh's Lawnmarket, the hub of Edinburgh's merchant establishment, and the baronial houses of an increasingly confident landed 'middling sort', such as Fyvie in Aberdeenshire or Seton and Lethington (later renamed Lennoxlove) in East Lothian, all built more for display than defence.

Wealth and status were flaunted in the architecture of the new chateaux and towerhouses set in generous landscapes, with wooded policies and shelterbelts, and in elaborately embellished and furnished interiors. The gardens of the wealthy demonstrated the taste, style and affluence of the building's owner, as a recently discovered panel from a painted ceiling (one of seven now on display at the Museum of Scotland) emphasises. The ceiling is thought to have been painted locally for an Edinburgh dwelling, Dean House, between 1580 and 1620 on wood imported from Scandinavia through Leith, Musselburgh or Inveresk. The ceiling panels divide into four biblical and three allegorical scenes, the latter 'personifying' the senses of Sight, Taste and Hearing (see pp. 2–3).

Interior decorative painting became all the rage after the Reformation, when painted ceilings (exceedingly rare in England) enriched the homes of nobles, lairds, merchants and craftsmen who, no doubt, looked out on elaborate gardens. Particular concentrations of ceilings appear in the east and this is not surprising, given our vigorous trade with the European seaboard. Near our east coast, where ideas and materials arrived on each tide, groups of decorative painters are known to have formed 'schools', particularly in Aberdeen and Edinburgh. Gardeners with gardening skills, plants, bulbs, tools, illustrations, and so on must have bonded with similar gusto into confederations, however informal. Just as we know the names of only a few gardeners, with few exceptions the painters remain anonymous. John Mellin, for example, has been linked with the ceilings at Delgatty Castle, Aberdeenshire, James Workman with Rossend Castle, Fife, and John Anderson with the decoration of the room in Edinburgh Castle where James VI is said to have been born. In Edinburgh in 1612, the Aberdonian John Anderson took as apprentice George Jamesone, who later created an ornamental garden in New Aberdeen. Here is a definite

link between decorative painting, the art of portraiture and the art of gardening.

Patrons of the painted ceilings and wall panelling that enlivened otherwise dull pinewood planks from the Baltic ranged from aristocrats like the Marquess of Huntly, who commissioned an emblematic ceiling and chapel painted with sacred subjects, and merchants like Sir George Bruce of Culross Palace where painted rooms are preserved today, to the tenant of Sailor's Walk, Kirkaldy, where the beams of the old house overlooking the harbour are painted with texts referring to the sea – 'They see his wonders in the deep' – and the garden might have had crushed-shell paths.

The decoration of the ceilings – with figurative or natural motifs and patterns outlined in geometric bold black lines and filled in with bright colours: blues, reds, ochres, greens and yellows – echoes the form of the popular and fashionable decorative knot garden: small, usually rectangular beds outlined with dwarf hedging such as box or rosemary, intricate, geometric and abstract, though sometimes (like the ceilings) representing imaginative objects such as heraldic beasts. The living green pattern-work knot was filled with gravels or coloured mineral substances or, if the design was open, the interstices were filled with plants. The consciousness that enjoyed elaborate decoration in the home desired to extend that sensitivity to its garden ground. If the subject matter of a painted ceiling was governed by the taste of the patron or the ability and imagination of the painter he or she employed, then the knots in the garden and what was planted in them were similarly devised.

What is a ceiling painting but a map of someone's inner world represented in the symbols and materials available? Painted wooden ceilings and panels were used both as domestic decoration and for the visual communication of scriptural and moral messages. Like a garden, a ceiling or painted panel could be 'read', its symbology immediately accessible to contemporaries. A sixteenth-century ceiling at John Knox House, Edinburgh, depicts a horned god and a female fertility symbol, or goddess, both with exaggerated sexual parts. What was going on there and at Prestongrange, East Lothian, where an even stranger ceiling was discovered in the 1960s, well preserved under a later plaster ceiling? Herbal potions were the province of the witches and warlocks

Mercury rules, with Flora below right, on the glorious Celestial Ceiling at Cullen. More than any other Renaissance artefacts, the painted ceiling symbolises Scotland's lost golden age. The Cullen ceiling was destroyed by fire in the late 1980s, shortly after its restoration by Stenhouse Conservation Centre.

Marc Ellington, Towie Barclay, Aberdeenshire (held at The Royal Commission on the Ancient and Historical Monuments of Scotland).

and a story told by Scotstarvit in *The Staggering State of Scottish Statesmen 1550–1650* is a reminder of the power of witchcraft in the lives of post-Reformation Scots who were gripped by witch mania. At Prestongrange 'the full force of the diabolical evil-eye expressions on the faces of the grotesques and fairies [on its painted ceilings] remain so unresolved and disconcerting' – and associated with occult practices, according to one commentator. This extraordinary painted ceiling, the earliest known in Scotland, dated 1581, was discovered at Prestongrange in 1962 and removed for safekeeping to Merchiston Tower in Edinburgh. It is one of the most expertly painted and iconographically interesting of all sixteenth-century ceilings. Contemporary ceiling designs generally hid symbols of the occult or the supernatural among innocuous images of decorative fruits and flowers, disguising magic as innocent fun, but the Prestongrange ceiling, far from being merely decorative, is 'pregnant with imagery, disconcerting in its curious juxtapositions, its fear and fascination with the unknown, the extra-sensory and the supernatural'.

The owner of Prestongrange, Mark Ker, became Earl of Lothian in 1606 and died in 1609, the victim, it is said, of witchcraft invoked by his wife Margaret Maxwell. Scotstarvit relates that Lady Lothian, who suffered from breast cancer, frequently kept company with wise women or witches. A well-known warlock called Playfair agreed to heal her if her affliction was transferred to someone she loved. Her husband, the Earl, said to be a 'lascivious adulterer', developed a growth on his throat which killed him. Meanwhile Playfair had been arrested under suspicion of the deed and locked up in Dalkeith Tower. The Earl's son obtained access to Playfair who was found strangled next morning with a sinister thin string tied round his neck, according to a practice of the time, so that there could be no suspicion of suicide. It has been suggested that the 2nd Earl of Lothian may have been the grand master of a coven since 'never more enquiry was made of the deed' and the family home was quickly disposed of.

Fertility symbols, horned gods, fairies and priapic Lucifer himself, offer a glimpse of Renaissance society far removed from the atmosphere suggested by the glassed-in fairy palace of green trimmings bound with birches, where James V took his ease at Atholl. But we should remember that Priapus was the God of Gardens, and

that even at this stage in garden history, gardens could mean different things to different people.

In sweet contrast, the goddess Flora was represented in other ceilings surrounded by stylised flowers in cultivation. Strawberries, plums, pears, grapes and fanciful birds and animals were embroidered on to decorative hangings, like the ones discovered in recent years, carefully preserved in trunks at Traquair House. Crewel work, popular for curtains and bed hangings, depicted a tracery of flowers originating in Kashmir, including exotics which would become available to Scottish gardeners during the next century.

Honeysuckle grows wondrously in the wild but carnations must be cultivated. Both flowers appear, entwined, in the 1595 portrait by an unknown artist of Esther Inglis (1571–1624), already a successful calligrapher in her twenties and about to be married. Are the flowers, delicately portrayed on the red background of the painting, hanging in the Museum of Scotland, real or imaginary? Were the honeysuckle flower and the carnation (symbols of love and devotion) cultivated by the enterprising Esther in her own garden? We will probably never know, but the portrait of this successful young Renaissance craftswoman is evidence that women played a part in the quickening pace of change in the sixteenth and seventeenth centuries, and were affluent in their own right.

The consciousness that created the ceilings and worked the embroideries and tapestries created the gardens of the time. Lowland Scotland's shortage of timber had led to the importation of Scandinavian and Baltic softwoods which lacked aesthetic quality and required enhancing. It is likely that the Continental penchant for ceiling painting was imported along with the wood itself. The colourful confidence of painted ceilings had appeal as an appropriate outward expression of the Scottish nation's growing prosperity, new learning and the strengthening of its alliances with Northern Europe and Holland. Gardens were equally expressive. The ceiling painters decorated bare wood; the gardeners decorated bare ground.

What is a garden but a piece of land reflecting someone's sense of order, design and ingenuity in obtaining materials and plants to make that garden unique, but of its time?

Professionals, craftworkers and merchants could now afford to build

Esther Inglis was already a successful calligrapher when her portrait was painted by an unknown artist, and a member of the rising 'middling sort' who wanted homes and gardens at the end of the sixteenth century.

Unknown artist. © The Scottish National Portrait Gallery, reproduced with permission.

homes with gardens and buy possessions previously only within the reach of traditional landowners. With the evidence gathered so far, it is possible to create an imaginary garden in the style someone like Esther Inglis might have aspired to.

In her portrait, Esther Inglis holds a book, said to be evidence of her trade of calligraphy. Like other craftspeople and patrons, she would have studied emblem books which were widely available in her time, and which had circulated throughout Europe since the fifteenth century. The books were a common source of decorative imagery – for painted wood, embroidery, tapestry and probably garden design too – and the meaning of the individual emblems was instantly recognisable, rather like 'logos' today. 'Emblems bring down intellectual to sensible

A Garden Design for Esther Inglis

A walled garden: modest not grand, divided into 'rooms' by paths running north–south, east–west, and by trellis fencing espaliered with apple trees, underplanted with thrift, periwinkle and wild strawberries. The 'rooms' are further divided by patterned box hedges or knots infilled with crushed sea-shells, flowers, including carnations, and herbs. Clipped bay trees or juniper form the centre of each of four knots. A tree or sundial is the central focus of the whole garden. The garden's enclosing stone walls retain heat, and encourage ivy, honeysuckle and fruit trees, pears and geans (cherries).

things; for what is sensible always strikes the memory stronger, and sooner impresses itself than the intellectual,' wrote Francis Bacon, who had 'a very full knowledge of the art of memory, and himself used it'.

You could select emblematic images according to the particular world view you wished to present. Conrad Gesner's two volumes, *Historiae Animalium* (1551) and *Icones Animalium* (1560), inspired the porcupine and the rhinoceros on the painted ceiling at Rossend Castle and many of the other animals that appear on Scottish painted ceilings. The source for the Rossend lion with a sword between its forefeet was made from Whitney's *A Choice of Emblemes, and other Devises* (1586) and an emblem book by Rollenhagen inspired the winged helmet, serpents and cornucopias. Unique Scottish influences appear in the form of heraldic motifs and patterns with Celtic sources at Huntingtower Castle and the bold geometric design of the ceiling at St Mary's, Grandtully, which matches the painted pattern for the barrel-vaulted ceiling in the 'heich hoose' at Moubray House in Edinburgh's Royal Mile; here George Jamesone, Scotland's first portrait painter, is known to have lodged. Covert religious symbols and the planets – Sun, Moon, Mercury, Jupiter, Mars, Venus, Saturn – were common motifs, gloriously represented – with Flora and Ceres – on the fabulous Celestial Ceiling at Cullen, (tragically destroyed by fire shortly after its

Date stone: 1676 and the entwined initials of the owners of a merchant's house at Culross.

© Sheila Mackay, 2001.

restoration in the 1980s). Celestial imagery celebrated the place of man (the microcosm) in the world (the macrocosm).

Editions of the same emblem book became available in several cities at different times, using the same printing blocks. They were a vital part of the kit available to decorators, and gardeners began to have guide books too, with illustrations of knots, mazes and points of husbandry. The fourth part of Seralio's *L'Architettura* (1537) contained the first printed designs for parterres in geometrical patterns. European garden design at this stage was stereotypical, easy to copy and still a craft, but a craft that showed signs of emerging as an art form.

By the end of the century, 'a delictible time of peax', as James VI's Privy Councillor put it, merchants like Bruce of Culross and nobles like David Lindsay, 10th Earl of Crawford, were enjoying leisure and pleasure applied to home, garden and surrounding landscape. Old families as well as the newly affluent had the energy to reinvent their spirituality and to design garden landscapes as a form of celebration and, therefore, of art. And gardens appeared in Scottish art, too.

The recent discovery of the panels from a barrel-vaulted ceiling

The seal of the ancient
Burgh of Culross.

Reprinted by permission of the
National Trust for Scotland.

by a local artist (1580–1620) for an Edinburgh dwelling, Dean House, is
of immeasurable importance to Scottish garden history and is evidence
of the style of formal gardens aspired to by owners of homes like the
chateaux noted by the Duc de Rohan. The style of the Dean House
painted panels is sophisticated, the colour vibrant, the content absorbing
– a local reflection of Renaissance Europe in a domestic setting, even
although statues and church windows dedicated to saints had been swept
away during and after the Reformation. The seven panels divide into two
groups of four and three. The first grouping depicts religious scenes: St
Luke, Abraham and Isaac, King David playing his harp, and Judith and
Holofernes. The second set of panels personify the senses of Sight,
Taste and Hearing. The Sense of Sight is represented by a woman
holding up a looking glass against the landscape of Edinburgh, the Castle
and Arthur's Seat; Taste brings a goblet to her lips against a backdrop of
a lake with a swan and a formal garden with a covered walk; Hearing
plays her lute with a deer looking on, and a castle in the background.

The 'Taste' panel is evidence, as the museum's description says,
of the Renaissance fashion for formal gardens. More importantly, the
artist or his patron has chosen to symbolise taste as a garden. Scots of

Opposite.
Culross Palace, Fife: George Bruce made a fortune from coal mining and salt panning so that by 1611 he could look south over the Firth of Forth through the lead–glazed windows with half–shutters of his fine mansion, and north over his terraced gardens.

Left.
Dumpie hens in the orchard divided from a small kitchen garden by a wattle fence.

Both © Sheila Mackay, 2001.

Opposite.
Decorative vegetables in raised beds divided by crushed-shell paths, one of which leads under the covered walkway.

Top.
Fennel, cabbage, spinach and globe artichokes: all the vegetables grown at Culross Palace garden today were available to sixteenth-century gardeners.

Bottom.
A stone wall divides the orchard and formal garden in the traditional manner.

good taste required a formal garden. Gardens were now regarded as an art form by the intelligentsia and no other Renaissance survival compares with the magnificently artful pleasaunce at Edzell Castle. Under the guidance of David, the 10th Earl, the pleasaunce his mother, Catherine, had known began to evolve into something glorious, a theatre for all the senses, that bridged the sixteenth and seventeenth centuries with peerless brio.

It is likely that the garden of Culross Palace was a traditional affair and similar to the garden the National Trust for Scotland has imagined and created for the house today, with its triumvirate: formal garden, orchard and vegetable and herb garden, surrounded by stout walls that protected against the ravages of the weather and animal predators rather than human invaders. This style of garden landscape, its three divisions reflecting the form of monastic gardens, remained popular in Scotland at least until the eighteenth century, its features at once graceful and utilitarian, demonstrating the intrinsic sense of its creator.

In the last decade of the century, George Bruce began to build a new house off the narrow cobbled streets that converge on the Mercat Cross at Culross, a religious centre since the sixth century, said to be the birthplace of St Mungo, patron saint of Glasgow. Bruce, a distant relative of Robert the Bruce, had been attracted to the burgh (one of the most complete examples of a seventeenth and eighteenth century burgh even today) by the prospect of making his fortune in coal and salt produced in the pans along the edge of the river. The monks, the first miners to exploit the coal seams under the Firth of Forth, had been defeated by the seepage of the sea into their works. George Bruce, however, invented apparatus to drain his coal mine that ran for a mile under the Forth, and it made him a fortune in his lifetime, before a storm destroyed the undersea mine in 1625, the year he died.

Coal, salt and other goods, including the baking girdles the burgh was famous for, were exported to Scandinavia in ships that brought back pantiles and wood as ballast. Eventually the thatched roofs of the burgh would be pantiled and the plain deal ceilings and panelled walls painted according to Scandinavian and other European traditions. The Culross houses on the edge of the harbour displayed Dutch influences and contained living quarters as well as acting as the

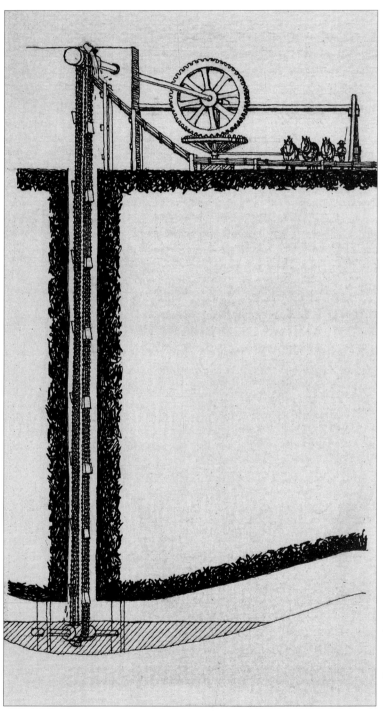

Artist's impression of the ingenious coal-draining apparatus devised by Sir George Bruce of Culross.

merchants' storage sheds. Local people called George Bruce's house Culross Palace because it was the grandest house of all; as well as traditional gardens, there were eight painted ceilings in the house when it was completed in 1611. But the house was built in two stages. Above a dormer window in the first range an inscription reads 'GB 1597' and in the freestanding second building 'SGB 1611' reflects the knighthood he received the same year.

In a high corner of the sloping garden a wooden seat under an arbour of white roses (*Rosa alba*) looks inviting. From here, the scent wafting from clumps of lavender, sage and thyme, there is a dramatic view of the back of the house. It is a gallant house, sturdy and straight-forward as the ships that plied the Forth which, in those days, came close to the house, kept back with a staunch wall as John Slezer depicted in an illustration for *Theatrum Scotiae*, 1693. On an overcast summer's day the Forth, viewed over the pantiled roofs of the house is mirror-still. Visitors come and go, like players on to a stage, into the theatre of the imaginary landscape the National Trust for Scotland has created. A black dumpie (a variety of hen known in Scotland for 900 years) cackles in the silence, then follows its cockerel mate on a tour of the orchard, enclosed by a wicker fence, where green apples bud on the trees:

> Now of all Grounds the orchard claims the Praise
> As most ressembling Antient Paradise.

So wrote Sir John Clerk of Penicuik more than a century after Culross had been built, but on a morning like this when the orchard does indeed suggest a glimpse of paradise, it is his words that spring to mind. Opposite the orchard the herb garden flourishes with fennel, fenugreek, and other culinary and medicinal herbs. Below the high terraces spreads the formal garden, divided by crushed-shell paths into raised beds of flowers and vegetables where white and yellow butterflies flit. Everything seen planted here would have been grown in Scotland in George Bruce's day.

We miss the things it is impossible to recreate, though we might imagine the bustle, the rough and tumble, the barter and cheek of loud-mouthed laundrymaids, cooks, labourers, scullions and grooms, coming and going in the Bruce family's service. The clatter of hooves,

Opposite, top.
Illustration from *Theatrum Scotiae* (1693) showing Culross Palace behind the estuary walls of the Forth.

Reprinted by permission of the National Trust for Scotland.

Opposite, below.
View of the Bass Rock from *Theatrum Scotiae* (1693).

Reproduced by permission of the National Library of Scotland.

93

horse, sheep, cows, on polished cobbles, the stench of sewage, silage and pig manure. Culross Palace today is an empty stage set with delightful properties, the garden with its traditional divisions and its buildings gloriously limewashed in deep ochre with red pantiled roofs. Nevertheless Culross Palace is the nearest we can come to realising what sort of home and garden a wealthy entrepreneur aspired to at the beginning of the seventeenth century after the Crowns of Scotland and England were united.

James VI and I promised to return again and again to Scotland, although he only came back once. When Mary, Queen of Scots, had entered Edinburgh in 1561, it was through an archway 'coloured with fine colours' where a child, stepping from a quatrefoil cloud, handed her the keys of the town. For the ceremonial entrance of her son James VI in 1579 'the fore-howsis of the streits ... war all hung with magnifik tapestrie, with payntit historeis, and with the effegeis of noble men and wemen.' The cloud had been replaced by a globe and at Salt Market Cross a painted decoration displayed the genealogy of the Kings of Scotland.

A King Charles spaniel patiently awaits the return of its owner, Culross.

© Sheila Mackay, 2001.

94

CHAPTER 7

Gardens for Delight's Sake

'HERE SHALL YE SEE NO ENEMY BVT
WINTER AND ROVGH WEATHER'

One of the great gardens of history evolved at Heidelberg Castle under the influence of Mary, Queen of Scots' grand-daughter, Elizabeth Stewart, after her marriage to Frederick V, Elector Palatine of the Rhine. The garden was talked about as an eighth wonder of the world.

For the London wedding in 1613, as Frances Yates writes:

> all the treasures of the English Renaissance were outpoured … Shakespeare was still alive and in London; the Globe theatre was not yet burned down; Inigo Jones was perfecting the court masque; Francis Bacon had published *The Advancement of Learning*. The English Renaissance was at a high point of splendour, developing into the dawning intellectual promise of the seventeenth century

And the Scottish court that had followed Elizabeth's father, James VI and I, to London in 1603 shared in that promise but left at home a peculiar vacuum. With the exception of a bit of tinkering here and there the royal gardens lay dormant after the 1603 Union of the Crowns. At Falkland in 1628 the new work of 'planting and contriving the garden anew' included the installation of a sundial, though no one held their breath.

In their inimitable way, though, Scots followed the pattern of the rest of Europe, and increasingly of England, in expressing all the 'airts'. John Anderson and George Jamesone had turned their hand to painting backdrops for court ceremonies and would do so again for the Edinburgh coronation of Charles I in 1633. The symbol of the globe had figured in James I's ceremonial entry into Edinburgh and there had been an established theatrical tradition well before Lindsay's *Ane Satyre of the Three Estaitis* was first performed for the court. Servants, scholars, travelling players and emissaries journeyed between the Palatine and London and Scotland. In this way, and through many other routes (Holland and France, for example), news and new publications percolated in many directions, but those who had not seen the Heildelberg garden at first hand would have to wait until 1620 to see the *Hortus Palatinus* by De Caus (Elizabeth's drawing master), published at Frankfurt, which included a detailed engraving of its

layout. Had the engraving of the garden not existed, we would not realise its breathtaking extent; the Palatinate garden, one the splendours of Jacobean Heidelberg, stood near the front line of battle at the outbreak of the Thirty Years War and was soon largely destroyed.

Elizabeth's brother, Prince Henry, had been deeply interested in Renaissance garden design: in mechanical fountains which could play musical tunes, in speaking statues and other extraordinary devices, the taste for which had been stimulated by the recovery of ancient texts describing such marvels by Hero of Alexandria and his school. The Prince employed the architect Inigo Jones and the garden-architect and hydraulic engineer Salomon de Caus, a French Protestant. Inigo Jones and De Caus were conspirators in the Renaissance revival of Vitruvius which based the arts and sciences on number and proportion (music, perspective, painting, mechanics and the like) and held that architecture was the queen of the mathematical sciences.

Inigo Jones's court masque scenery (1605–40) introduced to England Italianate concepts of planting, landscape and building – theatrical design intimately connected with architecture and its subsidiaries, perspective and mechanics. De Caus concentrated on garden design which had become closely affiliated to architecture and dependent, like architecture, on proportion, perspective and geometry, and on the latest refinements in mechanics for its decorative singing fountains and other embellishments. He followed Elizabeth to Heidelberg and began work on the castle and grounds as chief architect and engineer. He blasted away the rocky hillside and developed geometrical garden designs of great complexity on its smooth surface, high above the valley of the River Necker.

Like old castles and towerhouses in Scotland at the time, the ancient castle was modernised with new extensions, lightened with enlarged windows, and given a new designed landscape. 'Here, perched on a hillside in the heart of Germany, was an outpost of Jacobean England, a citadel of advanced seventeenth-century culture,' observes Frances Yates. In the castle gardens, grottoes enlivened with music from mechanical fountains appeared, caves contained mythological figures including Parnassus with the Muses, and Midas. When the sun's rays struck the statue of Memnon it sounded, just as it did in the

classical story. Magic – *scientific* magic – had entered the garden and the influential Scots in London knew all about it. One of them, Alexander Dicson 'the Scot', was closely associated with Philip Sidney, the leader of the Elizabethan poetic Renaissance. Bowes, the English representative at the Scottish court, had written to Lord Burghley in 1592, anglicising Dicson's name: 'Dickson, master of the art of memory, and sometime attending on Mr. Philip Sidney, deceased, has come to court.'

De Caus held music to be the chief of all the sciences. He is said to have constructed a water-organ (and to have developed its power from steam). This, with the sounds from his statues, fountains and grottoes, must have made Heidelberg as ' "full of noises" as Prospero's island', says Frances Yates. 'De Caus is clearly in the same theatrical atmosphere as Inigo Jones in his production of London masques [one of the most spectacular was for Elizabeth's wedding] …. Renaissance science, still involved in a magical atmosphere, began to use technical skills, on a large scale.'

Grand Scottish schemes utilised technical skills to some extent later in the century. Inigo Jones is thought to have had a hand in the modernisation of Glamis Castle by the Earls of Kinghorne. The 3rd Earl (who succeeded in 1646 and obtained a charter for the titles of Earl of Strathmore and Kinghorne, Viscount Lyon and Baron Glamis in 1688) created one of the four great Baroque gardens of Scotland at Glamis. Monarchic gardens no longer led the way. Ironically, at this time of stability the Scottish court, too hard up to improve architecturally, had little impetus to maintain the royal households in their former style. The important developments in landscape design were carried out on the estates of affluent aristocrats and in the new gardens and parklands of the rising 'middling sort' under the guidance of amateur and professional architects.

'HERE SHALL YE SEE NO ENEMY BVT WINTER AND ROVGH WEATHER,' declared the inscription above the entrance to the walled garden at Earlshall in Fife; you can still run your hand over the rough carved stone of it today.

A time of peaceful prosperity in the early seventeenth century had triggered Scotland's first building boom. The Crowns of England and Scotland had been united and throughout the century two new

The garden gate at Earlshall expressed the spirit of the age.

© Brinsley Burbridge, Royal Botanic Garden, Edinburgh.

professions – the law and the ministry – joined the 'middling sort' who required towerhouses, townhouses and tenements to match their swelling sense of self-esteem. Their demand stimulated the growth of another new profession – architecture. The Renaissance buildings of the sixteenth and seventeenth centuries, built in the native tradition, had displayed European and Irish influences, but after the Reformation gentleman-amateur and professional architects alike followed the great Baroque architect Sir William Bruce (c.1630–1710) in looking for inspiration south of the Border and touring England's country houses. A fervent Royalist, Bruce was knighted by Charles II after the Restoration of the Monarchy and appointed Overseer of the Royal Works in Scotland, which included the Palace of Holyroodhouse and much else besides. Bruce gave the profession of architecture an acceptable social face in Restoration Scotland and Sir John Clerk of Penicuik described Bruce as 'the introducer of Architecture into this country'. The coming taste was for the Baroque. Later in the century, Bruce would design the houses and formal landscapes at Balcaskie and Kinross and have a hand in many other developments including Tyninghame, Yester and Drumlanrig. John, 6th Earl of Mar (1675–1732), was one of the most gifted of the gentlemen-architects whose designs included the layout of grounds as well as architecture. Like Bruce's, their schemes emphasised the importance of the designed landscape in relation to the house.

Landscaped garden ground complemented gallant, evolving domestic towerhouses, some with near-legendary names like Crathes and Craigievar, superb examples of the ability of the lairds, the new feuars and the rising professions to create towerhouse symbols of a leisured class that could match or outshine the old families. There began to be a distinct rhetoric for the architecture and for the gardens of the different classes. Some would have their topiary, sundials, sweet-smelling arbours and formal knot-gardens like the artful gardens springing up all over Europe. Culross, Cawdor and Earlshall demon-strated straightforward walled gardens of this time. At this stage, although fruit trees were often still grown against the walls, the vegetables tended to be banished to distant parts of the garden and flowers were used to create complex geometric patterns on the terraces or within the walls. Every garden must both tame nature and reflect its

A superb example of baronial style, Scotland's finest contribution to European domestic architecture, Craigievar's exterior remains very much as it was in 1626, the year of its completion.

Reprinted by permission of the National Trust for Scotland.

The Long Gallery at
Crathes. The rising
'middling sort' of the
seventeenth century
created homes and gardens
that often matched or
outshone those of the
old families.

delights, bearing in mind the wild Scottish landscape and its 'terrible'
weather. In a country abundantly supplied with water and in love with
the sun, fountains seem to have come a poor second to sundials as a
central feature of the garden.

Monastery gardens avoided the shade on the sunny side of their
churches. The position of Renaissance gardens in relation to the sun
was crucial too and early Scots gardeners may even have conceived of
the house as an earthly representation of the sun itself. John Reid
would write (1683) that all walks, trees and hedges must radiate from
the house 'like the sun sending forth its beams'. To symbolise further
the house's umbilical link to the sun, the walls of the house were often
brilliantly limewashed with earth colours, a tradition revived in the
recent restoration of Culross Palace and at Kellie Lodging, Pittenweem, whose saffron walls zing out, even in the dreichest weather, as if
to echo the gnomon of a sundial casting blocks of light and shade
throughout the day. The Renaissance house stood firm at the centre of
an ordered microcosm and the lord or the laird stood at the centre of
the household just as 'the sun is centre of this world [macrocosm], and
the nose the centre of the face', as John Reid put it. The garden was
sited to catch the sun, to warm up 'the cold, chilled, baren, rugged-

natur'd ground in Scotland'. And no garden was complete without a sundial, both as a timepiece and as a reminder of the vital importance of the sun to everything that lives.

Holyrood Palace gardens are positioned to attract the sun from the moment it rises above the summit of Arthur's Seat until it sets over the Forth. At Edzell the garden was constructed on the south side of the towerhouse. High wall-faced sundials became popular on private and public buildings; sundials acted as centrepieces in formal parterres and on terraces. The Aberdonian, Davie 'Doo A' thing' Anderson, had 'devysit ane instrument of his own ingyne, to draw and mak dyellis or sone horolages' in 1596. This ingenious sundial may have been the inspiration behind the one that was in place at Holyrood for Charles I's return visit to Scotland in 1633. The King's master mason, John Mylne, was paid handsomely for this polyhedral sundial, whose invention was pioneered in Scotland and whose technology had been assisted by Napier's discovery of logarithms in 1614. The twenty-nine facets of the Holyrood sundial take the form of cavities of various shapes, each decorated with devices such as thistles and roses and the initials of King Charles and Queen Henrietta Maria. Each cavity contained a dial needle, and it was a wonder of the age that whatever time of day it was, each of the twenty-nine needles told the same time. Then, as now, people loved invention and the sundials caught on. Forty-seven free-standing polyhedral sundials are known to have graced Scottish gardens by the end of the century.

Sundials also celebrated the sun as God. Robert Fludd's cumbrously entitled *Ultriusque Cosmi, Maioris scilicet et Minoris, metaphysica, physica, atque technica Historis* covers the great world of the macrocosm, the universe, and the little world of man, the microcosm. As already mentioned, Fludd entered a double dedication to the first volume (1617) – on the macrocosm – first to God, and second to James VI and I as God's representative on earth.

A Lowland garden at Coltness Castle was modest yet innovative, as a unique and touching surviving account of 'middling sort' aspiration reveals. In 1654, Mr Thomas Stewart married and settled down to enjoy country life and in a few years to convert a small house, built for defence, into something 'modern' and suited to placid times:

It was agreed that, upon the marriage, the young folks should take up family in the country, and Cultness to be the place of residence [according to a contemporary account]. Mr Stewart applied himself to country affairs, and both husband and wife to their proper work in a retired life, and were full of beneficiency and Christian charity. He sett himself to planting and inclosing, and so to embellish the place.

Although parterres were popular, they held little appeal for more modest garden landscapers like Mr Stewart, whose garden 'lay to the south of the house on a slope falling to the west and was terraced into three cross levels by means of banks'. The level ground fronting the south of the house was a flower garden with a strawberry border; east and west of the house were cherry and nut gardens, edged with walnut and chestnut trees. A high stone wall south of the terraces was used 'for ripening and improving finer fruits' and formed the boundary wall of an orchard and kitchen garden 'with broad grass walks'. The remaining three sides were protected by a thorn hedge, dry ditch and shelterbelt. West of the house Mr Stewart created a nursery garden and a small plantation of birches, ash, sycamore and fir. North of the house a 4-acre grass sward had a corner fishpond stocked with pikes and perches. Taking in all its attributes, the designed landscape was a rectangle of 7 or 8 acres with the house near the centre.

As the century progressed, all over Scotland 'the middling sort' swelled with horticultural aspiration. Lairds, new feuars and up-and-coming professionals moved into fine homes with gardens. Many enjoyed intellectual, scientific and literary pursuits, collected books for their libraries, and were passionately interested in botany and gardening. A painted screen of pine and oak made for the home of advocate Robert Murray and his wife Christina Cowan, Wester Livilands House, Stirling, in 1629, on display at the Museum of Scotland, is a measure of 'middling sort' 'beneficiency and Christian charity'. The painter has adapted classical mythology for a Christian setting. Six sibyls or Ancient Roman prophetesses foretell the coming of Christ. The Murrays' garden near Stirling may well have matched the Stewarts' garden at Coltness.

At the other end of the scale, immense power and influence

Multifaceted sundial at Pitmedden Great Garden.

were the rewards of members of the aristocracy who followed the King to London or remained as his chosen representatives north of the Border. This ruling class amassed fortunes and strengthened its control through intermarriage. By the early eighteenth century status would be reflected by the grandeur of dwellings in designed landscapes. The 2nd Earl of Tweeddale, a privy councillor and commissioner of the Treasury, had been planting at Yester at least since the 1660s. The park was enclosed by 1676 and by the 1690s one of the most ornate formal gardens and one of the largest parks in Scotland had been laid out around the old sixteenth-century towerhouse that would become a great mansion in the classical style under the direction of James Smith (Bruce's successor in the office of Overseer of the Royal Works in Scotland) and Alexander MacGill (architect to the burgh of Edinburgh from 1720), and of William Adam and his sons, John and Robert, throughout the next century. A series of delightful oil paintings (1690s) usually attributed to Jacob de Witt (1640–97) accurately depict the gardens and landscape at Yester. Other contemporary commentators praised the gardens and the extravagant features shown in the paintings, a rectangular flat-walled garden divided into seven compartments lying to the south of the house. Beyond the garden gate lay the 'Wilderness', with an exuberant cascade falling down a steep bank into a broad canal.

Aristocratic Scots had, of course, great estates in England which influenced the development of their Scottish estates as well as those of the gardeners, designers and landowners who visited them. John Evelyn, the celebrated seventeenth-century connoisseur of trees and gardens, took an after-dinner walk in the Duke of Lauderdale's Ham House in 1678 and found the house and the garden 'inferior to few of the best Villas in Italy itselfe … [with] Gardens, orangeries, Groves, Avenues, Courts, Statues, perspectives, Fountains, Aviaries'. Evelyn was a friend of the 2nd Earl of Tweeddale and of the 6th Earl of Haddington who wrote that 'he was too credulous, and regarded the age of the moon too much, and other niceties too trifling for so grave a man.'

At a time of such expansion even the highest in the land had a great deal to learn about the art of Western gardening first invented by Egypt, Greece and Rome. Rich trove from the vigorous trading network with France, England, the Baltic and the Low Countries

A set of five estate surveys would have been unique even in England around 1685 when the second Earl of Tweeddale commissioned five views in oils of Yester House, East Lothian, attributed to Jacob de Witt (1640–97). One of these views from the most important surviving Scottish seventeenth-century house and garden surveys is shown here.

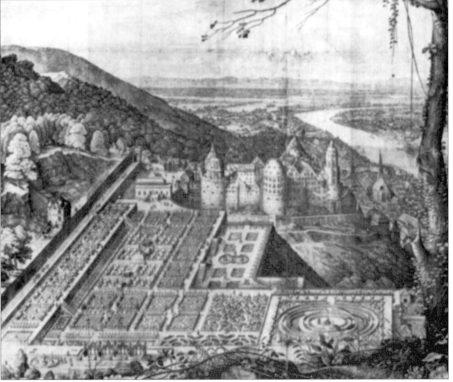

continued to infiltrate many strands of life, not least the decoration of homes and the creation of the new domestic gardens. Far from being dour, the creations of the privileged rejoiced in colour, texture and design. Visitors looking down from towerhouse, townhouse or tenement interiors in that golden age of prosperity enjoyed by the 'good and greit' before the Act of Union expected to see gardens to match.

Ideally, the garden could be seen and 'read' from the windows of the house; ideally, it would be a work of art. As far as possible house and garden should delight. Henry Peacham described the decorative form of Scottish painted ceilings in *The Art of Drawing* (1606) as 'an unaturall or unworldly composition for delight sake of man' containing 'beasts, birds, fishes, flowers etc. without (as wee say) Rime or reason'. He went on to say that representations of naked boys riding or playing with their paper-mills or bubble-shells upon 'Eagles, Dolphins, etc.' were acceptable images as were 'the bones of a Rammes head hung with strings of beads, with Ribands, Styres [satyres], Tritons, apes, cornucopias, cherries and any other inuention with a thousand more such idle toyes, so that herein you cannot be too fantastical'. Peacham's language suggests a world where there is far more than meets the eye. He also summons up an age of playful experiment which survived right to the end of the seventeenth century when a Dutch stonemason carved naked boys on dolphins, cornucopias and other delights to adorn the gate that leads out of Sir William Bruce's inspired garden at Kinross House (see p. 148).

Many amateur gardeners and plant lovers became serious botanists in the seventeenth century, avidly collecting new plants for their gardens. New exotic bulbs were sought after, scarlet lilies *(Lilium chalcedonicum)*, narcissi, hyacinths and prized tulips. In 1637 the tulip 'Viceroy' was advertised for 3 000 florins (around £1 500 today), an example of 'tulipomania', the speculative trade in buying and selling – and stealing – 'breeder' bulbs. Scented jasmines came in from Asia via Spain and New World flowers appeared: African marigolds, sunflowers, trailing nasturtiums (*Tropaeolum majus*). The scientific age embraced its bride, horticulture, and celebrated with a rush of florilegia (printed collections of living ornamental plants), how-to manuals, botanical gardens, nurseries, and all manner of inventions

Top.
Turk's cap lilies have been grown in the Edinburgh Botanic Garden since the seventeenth century.

© Deni Bown; from *Four Gardens in One* by Deni Bown and Alan Bennell, The Stationery Office Books, 1992.

Bottom.
A detailed engraving of the Palatinate Garden at Heidleberg published by De Caus in the *Hortus Palatinus* (1630). The garden was regarded as a wonder of the age.

Frances Yates, *The Rosicrucian Enlightenment*, Routledge & Kegan Paul, 1972.

including greenhouses, stove houses and frames. Lists of plants grown in the famous London garden of the John Tradescants, father and son, provided a record of most plants known at the time which could be grown successfully in northern Europe. The Bishop of London grew plants experimentally at Fulham Palace and made these available to the nurseries springing up everywhere, including Scotland. Horticulturists soon realised that the temperate British climate had advantages which allowed many plants from a variety of habitats to survive without special protection or culture. Plants that did need protection were cultivated in structures called greenhouses and conservatories, so named by John Evelyn. Oranges, lemons, myrtles, bays, jasmines and other tender plants were grown in large pots. London's Brompton Park Nursery held a stock of 40 000 plants by the end of the seventeenth century.

In the north gardeners had to discover what could be cultivated in their cold, chilled ground. From its magnificent position on the shores of the Pentland Firth, the Castle of Mey commands lands that once belonged to the Bishops of Caithness. In 1567 George Sinclair, the 4th Earl of Caithness, built the Z-plan tower and two walled gardens were added; the older west garden was described as 'greenfaced gardens' in 1628 by William Lithgow. Although the exact date of the garden walls is uncertain, another eighteenth-century account describes 'plenty of apples strawberries and cherries prospering within its bounds despite the harsh climate'.

Further west and with a milder climate than other parts of the exposed Caithness coastline, the valley setting of the Kyle of Tongue was chosen as the seat of the Clan Mackay, my forebears, described as 'battered warriors' in the *Book of Mackay*. Yet they were given to finer things; in 1650 the Chieftain, Lord Reay, had a 'brilliant' wife, 'a green historian a smart poet the mirror of our north bred ladyes'. The present Tongue House and garden walls are dated 1678. The magnificent mountains of Ben Loyal and Ben Hope transmute to rolling hill pastures above the house and its sheltered, turned-in garden landscape. The sea loch waters either roar against or caress the shoreline skirting Tongue House's walls, now the home of the Countess of Sutherland. Here was a place to recover from skirmishes and wars. The house is thought to have been destroyed by fire under

the troops of General Monck during the Civil War. As at Castle of Mey there are two walled gardens and the smaller garden, now a drying green, may have been an orchard. The home of the seventeenth-century Countess of Sutherland, Dunrobin Castle, was 'a house well seated upon a mote hard by the sea in a pleasant garden planted with all kinds of froots, hearbs and floors used in this kingdom', according to Sir Richard Gordon, a contemporary historian.

Parts of Scotland had a favourable climate for many new varieties; some, unhappy in England, would settle well on the Gulf-warmed Scottish west coast. Through trial and error, the perennials, woody plants and climbers that would succeed were discovered, so that by the second half of the century the flow of new plants transformed the appearance and potential of gardens and parklands. Parkland surrounded by unimproved nature began to be appreciated as much as formal pleasure gardens. The common parkland tree species used were ash, beech, birch, oak, sycamore and Scots pine or 'firr'. Only oak trees remain today from this period of planting when small avenues were constructed to extend beyond the immediate surroundings of the house through areas of landscape, trees and grassland cunningly contrived to accentuate the beauty of the countryside and to emphasise the stature of the house.

Change was afoot but the fifteenth- and sixteenth-century vision of gardens as 'pleasaunces' persisted. Earthly paradises, on however small a scale, emulated elements of royal and aristocratic gardens of the previous century in terraces, parterres, garden pavilions and the like. John Parkinson (1567–1650), the English apothecary, gardener and herbalist, published his influential *Paradisi in Sole Paradisus Terrestris* (1629) – 'Park-in Sun's Park on Earth', the title a pun on his own name – with a frontispiece illustrating a Garden of Eden and carrying a dedication to Henrietta Maria, wife of Charles I. The book, devoted to plants for 'a garden of delight and pleasure', would be well known to Scots horticulturalists. In his *Paradisus*, Parkinson advocates open knots, 'proper' for 'outlandish' flowers arriving in Britain including daffodils, fritillarias, hyacinths, 'saffron-flowers' [crocus], lilies, tulips, anemones and French cowslips or 'beares eares'. He preferred box hedging for the form of the knot though conceded that 'lead, boards,

bones, tiles or pebbles' might substitute, and provided diagrams of over-and-under interlacing bands. Scotland made its own interpretations and by the middle of the century 'knot' had become a general term for the quarters of a square flower garden, intersected by walks at right angles. Scots would have approved of the focus of Parkinson's imagination: the flower garden, the kitchen garden and the orchard.

'Gardings' and 'orcheyards' were commonplace in Scotland. Sir William Brereton 'passed very many seats of the nobles and found good apple and other fruit trees, walnuts and sycamores' between Dunbar and Edinburgh in 1635. Rothiemay mentions gardens and orchards, as well as dwelling houses 'cleanlie and bewtifull and neat' in his description of New Aberdeen which he depicted in 1661:

> closses, lanes, and streets, have not been at first chaulked out
> or designed by any geometricall rule. The buildings of the
> toune are of stone and lyme, rigged above, covered with slaits,
> mostlie of thrie or four stories hight, some of them higher.
> The streets are all neatlie paved with flint stone, or a gray kind
> of hard stone not unlike to flint. The dwelling houses are
> cleanlie and bewtifull and neat, both within and without, and
> the syde that looks to the street mostlie adorned with galleries
> of timber, which they call fore-stairs. Many houses have their
> gardings and orcheyards adjoyning.

Even allowing for artistic licence in Rothiemay's depiction of the gardens of Edinburgh's Canongate (1647), the ingenuity and diversity of their designs is astonishing. In map form, the gardens resemble glorious carpets rolled out as in an Eastern market, the finest examples, of course, spread beside the palace and abbey of Holyroodhouse. If, by 1647, the gardens had achieved such a degree of sophistication (parterres and knots in diverse designs, culinary gardens and trees), without a doubt they had been established many years before.

The first Scottish book on the subject, *The Scots Gard'ner*, appeared in 1683 with the rider 'Published for the Climate of Scotland' and *The Gard'ners Calendar*, 'Shewing in each Moneth When to performe the particulars, &c. What Garden dishes and drinks are in season'. And

John Parkinson's influential *Paradisi in Sole Paradisus Terrestris*, published in 1629, carried a frontispiece illustrating a Garden of Eden and a dedication to Henrietta Maria, wife of Charles I.

© Royal Botanic Garden, Edinburgh.

there is an empathetic note for the 'Reader': 'The Gard'ners year is a circle as thier labour, never at an end.'

A random example from the calendar reveals a great deal about the produce expected from the kitchen gardens of Scots affluent enough to sustain them:

> MAY: Coleworts and other Herbes, (being eaten with
> contentement is better than a fatted Ox without it) Sage (with
> Butter), Leeks, Parsly, Thuyme, Marjoum, Sorall, Spinage, &c
> … Early Cherries, Straw-berries, near the end [of the month].
> Cyder, Metheglin, Liquorish Ail, &C.

Here is a comprehensive manual, packed with information, much of it specific, about propagating plants, forest trees and fruit trees, and cultivating and preparing ground. The first part of the book 'treats of Contrivance' and includes practical advice on designing and laying out gardens, levelling ground, making avenues and walks, planting thickets and orchards, making the kitchen garden and making a pleasure garden. The book tells us that Scottish gardens, sophisticated in John Reid's day, must have been so far earlier. Reid was born at Niddry Castle, near Winchburgh, where his grandfather and father were both gardeners. He worked on 'the celebrated gardens of Hamilton' and at Drummond Castle with its extensive gardens in the Italian, French and Dutch styles. At Lawers, or Fordie, in Perthshire, where he is thought to have been head gardener, he started writing his book. The year of its publication found him at Shank, the East Lothian estate belonging to the Lord Advocate of Scotland, Sir George Mackenzie of Rosehaugh, infamous as 'the Bluidy Mackenzie', partly from his zeal in pursuing the Covenanting followers of Richard Cameron. John Reid decided to emigrate with his family to an American colony in New Jersey being promoted in Edinburgh, even before *The Scots Gard'ner* rolled off the printing press of David Lindsay of Heriot's Bridge. There, at the settlement of Perth Amboy, Reid exercised his proficiency at laying out new estates in the post of Deputy Surveyor-General.

John Reid's advocacy of paths, walks and trees radiating from the house translated well to grand gardens, but the walled garden enshrining the three traditional divisions of the Middle Ages –

orchard, vegetable garden and flower garden – each in its walled enclosure, suited the Scottish climate and sensibility and would retain its popularity for at least two centuries. A garden filled with flowers to delight the sights of sense and smell, with herbs to enhance food and cure maladies, vegetables and fruits overflowing in kitchen and pantry – what more could a modest Scot want?

Towerhouse gardens also functioned as formal pleasances or outdoor rooms with separate or contained areas for herbs and vegetables within their walls. Townhouses and tenements, too, had garden lands or rigs filled with herbs, flowers and vegetables grown within geometrically shaped plots and bordered with box-lined paths, often with an adjoining orchard. In orchards, pear (not luscious, but for the kitchen), apple and cherry trees were commonly grown, as they had been in monastic gardens. St Mary's Pleasance at Haddington, East Lothian, has a lovely recreated seventeenth-century orchard today, glorious in late spring. Plum trees were less common and peach and apricot trees were only found in gardens whose owners could afford to provide heated sheds or other warming devices. The wild strawberry was widespread and jostled with red and white currants, gooseberries and raspberries – soft fruit mainstays – and beds of herbs, vegetable plots and composted flower beds displaying annuals like hollyhocks and sunflowers. Not far from Holyrood Palace today, at Dunbar's Close in Edinburgh's Royal Mile, a recreated seventeenth-century garden displays beds of thyme and lavender surrounding trimmed bay trees, rosemary, roses, a fig tree on an ancient wall adjoining the Canongate Kirk and espaliered apple trees underplanted with thrift.

These days, now that summer has arrived, my outdoor room is this garden, about the size of a tennis court, its core divided into two knot gardens on one side of the path, with enclosed bays displaying flowers on the other. On warm days after rain, the air is perfumed with lavender, roses, bay and thyme. People wander in and out of the garden, like actors on a stage: courting couples, office workers on a lunch-time break, down-and-outs, one with a tartan cap attached to a red wig which he keeps in his pocket ready to put on in case he has to pose for tourists' cameras. Blackbirds fly in and out of the four conical bay trees at the centre of small knots edged with privet, surpassing the songs of other birds. Here is a sensuous feast for eyes, nose and ears, as close an

ARLY
SCOTTISH
GARDENS

approximation in size to Mr Sutherland's first physic garden (established behind Holyrood Palace, less than a mile away) as anyone could hope to find three centuries later, a fitting place to review what I know of the Pleasaunce at Edzell and to plan my forthcoming visit.

An imaginative reconstruction by John Knight showing how the terraced gardens at Aberdour Castle might have looked in the seventeenth century.

Historic Scotland.

CHAPTER 8

'Paradisi in Sole'

AROUND THE FABRICK SPREAD THE WIDE PARTERRE

LIKE TO A VERDANT MANTLE EDGD WITH GOLD

The small but growing horticultural elite knew about the elaborate designed landscapes of Italy and France. They too began to regard gardening as an art form, perhaps the most important of all, since in the design of the land the other arts met. Painters, architects, sculptors, poets and philosophers gave their minds to the possibilities of the form and the perfecting of its practice. Men who excelled in the art of garden design – De Caus was one – were sought after and 'became the confidants of statesmen and the friends of kings'.

David Lindsay had elevated his walled garden, or 'pleasaunce', into an art form by 1604, an astonishing creative achievement whose importance is impossible to exaggerate. Here was a man who exhibited to the full *the* outstanding quality of Renaissance man – imagination. David Lindsay was cultured and well travelled. He studied in Paris, he was a Knight Templar, he spent his honeymoon at Nuremberg where he visited the studios founded by Albrecht Dürer. He employed the Germans, Bernard Fechtenburg and Hans Ziegler, 'Citiner of Nuremberg', to supervise extensive mineral mining works at Edzell where furnaces were constructed, and I don't think it is far-fetched to

Right.
Plan of the Pleasaunce at Edzell showing the position of the bas-reliefs.

Opposite.
Measured drawing of the Pleasaunce wall.

'Plan of Pleasaunce', Fig. 11, and 'Measured Drawing of Pleasaunce wall', Fig. 12, from *Publications of the Clan Lindsay Society*, Vol. V, 1977.

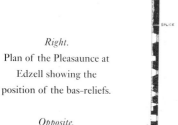

PLANETARY DEITIES

LIBERAL ARTS

GARDEN

CARDINAL VIRTUES

GROUND PLAN

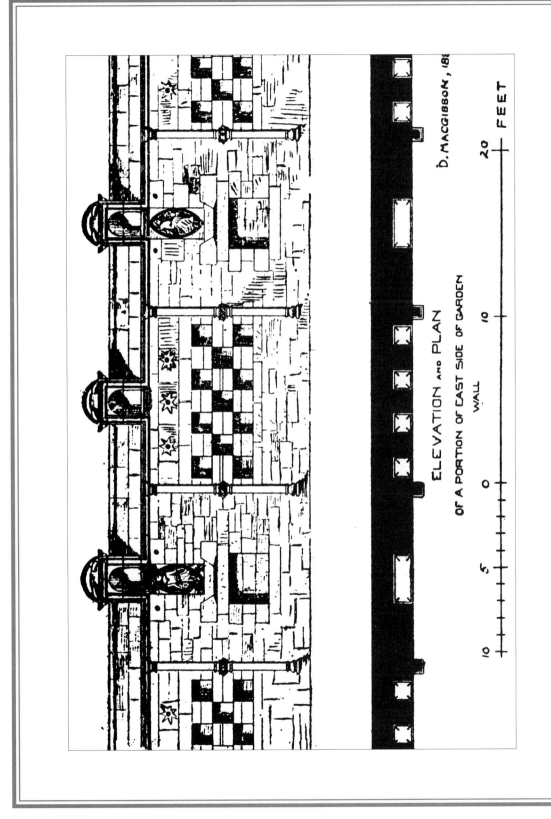

ELEVATION and PLAN
OF A PORTION OF EAST SIDE OF GARDEN
WALL

D. MACGIBBON, 188

10   5   0   10   20   FEET

suppose that Lord Lindsay would have used their skills to create Heidelberg-type features in the Pleasaunce: a musical fountain, perhaps, or a speaking statue.

Lindsay must also have met or at least heard of the apothecary and botanist at Nuremberg, Basil Besler (1561–1629), who had charge of the celebrated ornamental garden at Eichstatt for the Prince-Bishop. In 1600 the Prince-Bishop – an avid collector whose aim was to grow every plant known at the time – commissioned Besler to prepare the lavishly illustrated catalogue, *Hortus Eystettensis,* which appeared in 1613. Certainly Lindsay's travels stimulated his ideas for Edzell. Dürer's studios are known to have inspired the designs for the sculpted walls whose function was to stimulate the mind as well as the senses. At Lindsay's Edzell we stand in the Reformation. Some follow Protestantism, others cling to Catholicism. No wonder many of the intelligentsia embraced the refuge of Hermeticism.

I have described my first visit to the Pleasaunce at Edzell in the preface to this book. This time I bring with me a very little, but precious knowledge, culled from Dame Frances Yates's *The Art of Memory*. Camillo and his Memory Theatre, alluded to in a previous chapter, led to the thought that Lindsay's Pleasaunce had been a memory garden based on the Seven Pillars of Wisdom. Appendix 1 includes detailed extracts from Frances Yates's work and a section from

Right.

The first rung of Giulio Camillo's memory theatre based on *L'Idea del Theatro*, showing the Seven Pillars of Wisdom, symbolic of stable eternity. The planets and Apollo as the Sun God are represented on the second rung. The note below Apollo refers to the Golden Bough and 'intelligible things'.

From *The Art of Memory* by Frances Yates, Pimlico, 1992.

Opposite.

Mars resplendent in German armour after the engraving of Dürer's companion, George Pencz. Seven engravings were eventually recreated as the sculptures of the planetary deities on the East Wall of the garden at Edzell Castle.

'Mars', Fig. 20, from *Publications of the Clan Lindsay Society*, Vol. V, 1997.

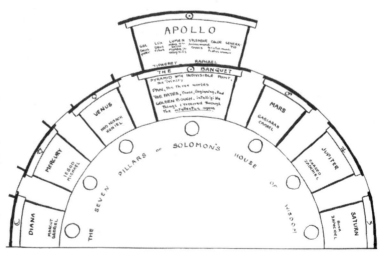

Wagner Garden Carpet

Courtesy of Glasgow Museums: The Burrell Collection

Dean House Panels – *Sight Personified,*
Hearing Personified and *Taste Personified*

Northfield House

Celestial Ceiling at Cullen

Bee-Boles at Kellie Castle

© Brinsley Burbridge, Royal Botanic Garden, Edinburgh

Mars, Wall of Planetary Deities, Edzell

© Sheila Mackay

Traquair Embroidery, Traquair House

Esther Inglis, Unknown Artist

Courtesy of The Scottish National Portrait Gallery

Inscription, Earlshall

© Brinsley Burbridge, Royal Botanic Garden, Edinburgh

Blairadam

The Pineapple

Yester House, Unknown Artist

Blair Castle by Colin Baxter

Lion: House of Dun, plasterwork by Joseph Enzer (1742–3)

Camillo's Memory Theatre is reproduced here. Hopefully others will explore further the link between Camillo's Memory Theatre and, later, Bruno's and Fludd's memory systems, and the Pleasaunce at Edzell, with input from the *Thamus* of Alexander Dicson 'the Scot'. Meanwhile the appendix sets down clues that lead to Camillo and on to Bruno, Fludd, Ramus and Dicson, and thence to the astonishing possibility that David Lindsay believed in the power of an occult memory system to magically activate pictures or sculptures through the imagination. As Frances Yates writes:

> The personified powers of the soul who conduct the reform of the heavens are JUPITER, JUNO, SATURN, MARS, MERCURY, MINERVA, APOLLO … these figures perceived inwardly in the soul are said to have the appearance of statues or pictures. *We are in the realms of the occult memory systems based on magically animated 'statues' as memory images.* [my italics]

The sculptures could be 'read' as well as responded to emotionally by contemporaries. The sun is God, Luna appears with watery Neptune. 'The affective or emotional appeal of a good memory image … is present in such images, expressive of the tranquillity of Jupiter, the anger of Mars, the melancholy of Saturn, the love of Venus.' The other walls are equally important: the Liberal Arts and the Cardinal Virtues. In both Protestantism and Catholicism, 'the Cardinal Virtues' have their opposite, 'the Cardinal Vices'; the 'liberal arts' are full of *double entendres* and open to various interpretations. With German engineers to hand working on his mining ventures, with a plentiful supply of water from the North Esk river, it seems likely that David Lindsay would have harnessed skills and materials to create some hydraulic device: a musical fountain, perhaps, scientific yet magical.

A suitable twenty-first-century celebration of the miracle that Edzell's sculpted walls remain (though some of the figures are replicas cast by Historic Scotland) would be the creation of a new garden design, bearing in mind 'The things that are built should guide and dominate what is planted' (Baccio Bandinelli). Twenty-first-century Scottish engineers might devise a water-organ, or a singing sculpture or fountain in emulation of the Heidelberg garden. The horticulture

A Garden Design for Edzell

The wall directly below the window of the Stirling Tower, the wall of the Christian Virtues, is skirted by two parallel paths of crushed sea-shells. One path is a covered walkway leading to the bath-house, a laburnum pergola; the other path, between the covered walk and the walls, allows the images on the walls to be enjoyed and studied privately. Similarly, broad paths lead from the entrance gate, edge the other two embellished walls of the planetary deities and the liberal arts, and the unembellished north wall. The *fez cheque* planting boxes, staged in sevens on each of the sculpted walls, are planted as they are at present: with blue lobelia and white alyssum. The laburnum pergola leads into a short curved avenue of hornbeam, thus linking the north wall which supports three generous turf seats along its length. There, facing the sun, is a semi-circular herb garden including rosemary, parsley, sage, marjoram, thyme, basil and mints, variegated in foliage and flavour and arranged in seven sections within knots of box hedging. The perfumed area is shielded from the strong sun and from the rest of the garden by stately taller things: angelica, fennel, lovage, basil, dill, thistles. In the centre, though, stands a mechanical statue representing Memnon. When the sun hits it at noon the statue sings.

The central rectangular lawn is divided by cruciform paths of crushed sea-shells: in each quadrant an artful parterre of box against a background of coloured earth and bands of turf, copied from Hans Vredeman de Vries's pattern book (*Hortorum viridariorumque elegantes et multi plicis formae*, 1583). As de Vries recommended, the parterres are intended to display exotic new plants. At the garden's centre, a seven-faced sundial, made of local sandstone. The cruciform walks are entered under latticework arbours displaying climbing roses. In front of the banqueting house, a fountain plays in an ornamental pool.

and floriculture of the garden require to be rethought to complement the gallant walls. Elements might be adopted from the designed landscape at the delightful St Mary's Pleasance at Haddington, East Lothian, a garden recreated in seventeenth-century style under the guidance of the late Sir George Taylor, a former director of Kew Gardens. Flowers, herbs and trees known to have been grown in seventeenth-century Scotland flourish there. Equipped with facts about David Lindsay's life, knowledge of seventeenth-century European garden design and catalogues of available plants, it is possible to hazard a plan for a reconstructed garden at Edzell Castle. As we know, it was a sine qua non of contemporary landscape design that the new garden must be 'read' for its beauty, art content and symbology from high windows overlooking it. The place to begin the imaginative process, then, is one of the long, glassless windows of Edzell Castle's Stirling Tower.

'Tulipomania' was rife in Holland – 'tulips to delight your eyes, with glorious garments, rich and new', enthused John Rea, author of *Flora, Ceres and Pomona ... or a complete Florilege, furnished with all requisites belonging to a florist* (1665). After all, he added: 'a choice collection of living beauties, rare plants, flowers and fruit, are indeed the wealth, glory and delight of a garden, and the most absolute indications of the owner's ingenuity; whose skill and care is chiefly required in their choice, culture and position.'

Lindsay would have had as many varieties to choose from as any European of his station. Rea recommended delights such as rose trees grafted to supply different colours in flower at the same time, auriculas, red primroses, hepaticas, double rose campions, double nonesuch, double dame's violet, 'the best wallflowers', double stock gillyflowers, and many other possibilities. Parterre beds might be planted with flowers that 'answer' each other: crown imperials, martagons (mountain lilies) and other tall plants in the corners, and 'tufts' of peonies surrounded by 'dwarf things' like anemones, ranunculi, tulips or irises. A rose hedge might be traced against lattice work under-planted with crocuses, with the greens and pot plants standing in front in the Dutch style.

Against the gorgeous dusky pink backdrop of his walls, or in specially prepared parterres, David Lindsay would have wanted to grow some of the 'exotick' and 'forraign' plants arriving in Britain in his own evolving garden ground. We know that he was au fait with European developments in garden design, that he was wealthy enough to import what he fancied into his pleasaunce. He would have been in touch with the outstanding horticulturalists of the day, in Europe and Britain, a man of his times, avidly interested in the arts as well as the new sciences.

And then, too, there is the possibility that the Lindsay women reigned in the garden, at least on the horticultural side. The Scottish court's move to London in 1603 had far-reaching political and economic consequences, not least of which was the new prominence of upper-class women, left behind to manage the estates when their husbands followed the King to London, as Deborah Howard points out. Noblewomen had little opportunity to travel. On account of the poor state of the country roads, which were still only passable on foot or on horseback, women were often marooned on their rural estates for long periods, especially during their child-bearing years. Some noblewomen became successful entrepreneurs in both coal mining and salt panning, and supervised the construction of estate buildings, schools and almshouses. Great households, as in England, had few resident female servants apart from nurses and washerwomen. In the towns, widows were in charge of many households and some women burgesses set up their own businesses as laundresses or caterers.

Newly affluent Scots as well as old families might also assert their sense of self-esteem by commissioning portraits from George Jamesone (1589/90–c.1644), who lived for a time in Edinburgh. The Aberdonian's career flourished from around 1620 (when easel paintings were still unusual in Scotland) with commissions from the nobility (many of whom were often in Edinburgh and kept houses there), scholars and leading burgesses. A random sample from the catalogue of his work turns up the 8th Earl of Argyll, Sir Thomas Burnett of Leys, Sir Robert Campbell of Glenorchy, Sir William Forbes of Craigievar, Mary Erskine, Countess Marischal, the 3rd Earl of Haddington and Dr Patrick Dun.

As George Jamesone's status grew, he acquired property in his native Aberdeen as well as farmlands and buildings at Fechil north of the city and part of the estate of Craighall. He also successfully

A Garden Design for George Jamesone

A four-square area enclosed by a low stone dyke, drained, well manured and divided into four rectangular parterres by cruciform paths of crushed sea-shells. The garden is entered through a wooden gate set under a lintel carved with the date '1635'. The pattern for the parterres is taken from Pictish or Celtic designs, traced in clipped box. Coloured gravels infill the background, and small knots infilled with lavender, thyme, sage, sea-pinks and cotton lavender surround the garden pavilion (perhaps a small theatre), set in the centre of the garden. Wooden seats outside, set near the sweet-smelling knots, invite the visitor to stay awhile. It is a circular pavilion, of rustic construction in thick pine imported from Scandinavia with a rough-slate conical roof. Seven windows (one for each planet) offer different perspectives of the garden (open windows, with shutters that can be closed against inclement weather). The vivid paintings inside are of the planetary deities, the technique similar to those used by decorative painters at Cullen, for example. The rays of the gilded ceiling roundel suggest the sun, 'Sol', to whom the pavilion is dedicated.

The 'well of Spa' provides water for a small ornamental pond where ducks and moorhens swim among rushes, as well as the central fountain on the axial path west of the pavilion. The fountain is balanced to the east by a polyhedral sundial devised by Jamesone's fellow Aberdonian Davie 'Doo A' thing', though less elaborate than the one Davie created for Holyrood.

petitioned the Town Council for land called Playfield, 'whair comedies were wont to be atit [acted] of auld besyde the well of Spa'. The area was 'spoilled, brockin, and cariet away be speat and inundation of watter'. It was a four-square field, a former theatre, which as James Gordon of Rothiemay's translator describes, was transformed into 'a gardyne for pleasur by the industrie and expense of George Jamesone,

The painter, George Jamesone, created a garden on the site of an old theatre ground at Playfield, Aberdeen.

ane ingenious paynter quho did sett up therin ane timber hous paynted al over with his owne hand'. Duncan Thomson comments that Jamesone's creation of the ornamental garden was an activity with a Flemish, even a Rubensian, ring to it.

Rubens's garden in Antwerp was subdivided into four rectangular parterres, surrounded by a low hedge. Enclosed gardens rooms were swept away and replaced with open, symmetrically laid, four-sided beds planted with clipped bushes (box and yew) and decorated with sculptures, fountains, ornamental pools, and parterres in complex geometric designs. During the Flemish Renaissance round or polygonal bowers formed by a tree pruned in layers and supported by a framework of small columns began to appear in gardens and public squares (a feature still common in Mediterranean gardens today). But we have very few details of Jamesone's garden which Arthur Johnston's series of Latin verse *Encomia Urbium* (1642), a poem in praise of New Aberdeen, mentions:

> Inde suburbanum Iamesoni despicis hortum
> Quem domini pictum suspicor esse manu.
> [From there you view Jamesone's suburban garden,
> Painted, I would guess, by the master's hand.]

On Jamesone's death, David Wedderburn, schoolmaster of Aberdeen, referred in his obituary to 'the skill of a hand that emulated the Flemings and the Italians'. It seems doubtful that Jamesone travelled beyond his own country, but bearing in mind his garden, it may be significant that John Michael Wright, painter at the court of Charles I, had been Jamesone's pupil several years earlier, when he took on the tenancy of the 'heich hoose' of Moubray House, in Edinburgh's Royal Mile. Even if Jamesone had not seen great English and European gardens of the period for himself, he would have heard about them and seen illustrations of them through contacts like Wright and the Earl of Tweeddale, who in addition to Yester had Tweeddale Court, opposite George Jamesone's lodgings at Moubray House, where he planted an avenue of lime trees on the Cowgate elevation. Jamesone's clients, made up of aristocrats and the 'middling sort', must have talked of their gardens during sittings, and having risen from craftsman to a member of

the middling sort himself, the artist may have visited their estates.

Gardens were regarded as an art form by middling sort 'in the know', and it was appropriate that Jamesone should spend some of his money and talent on his own suburban garden. The word 'suburban' used by Wedderburn suggests the Italian 'villa suburbia', which in Tuscany had become domestic rather than monumental a century earlier. Jamesone built in his garden a painted timber house – a suburban pavilion. Bearing in mind the wet Scottish climate and the paint materials available to him, the timber house must have been painted inside ... or so I think.

At Gaillon, overlooking the Seine, a large wooden pavilion housed a marble fountain imported from Italy; the Villa Lante has two wooden pavilions dedicated to the Muses. Garden galleries (the wooden gallery was a feature of Scottish Renaissance architecture) in European gardens overlooked parterres and often terminated in pavilions. It would be outlandish to suggest that Jamesone's 'timber hous' was on a par with pavilions set in significant European gardens, but, given the artist's talents, experience and contacts, his is certain to have been superior to a garden shed. As we weave together facts and hints and guesses, an imaginary landscape begins to emerge on the site George Jamesone purchased at Playfield, Aberdeen, with the added refinement of a riveting new clue:

> **Theatre:** The garden theatre is one of the most attractive inventions of the Italian Renaissance ... Perhaps the most charming is that of the Villa Marlia near Lucca (late 17th c) in yew, with footlights and prompter's box in *Buxus sempervirens* (box); even when not in use this theatre conjures up imaginings and thus justifies itself as a permanent garden decoration ... *as a garden folly it can scarcely be equalled* [my italics]. (*Oxford Companion to Gardens*)

It makes sense; Jamesone might well have had a theatre in his timber house. The very name Play-field means an open-air theatre – 'whair comedies were wont to be atit [acted] of auld' – and it seems reasonable to suppose that George Jamesone, imbued as a Renaissance artist with a love of all the arts, and with his experience of making props for

theatrical spectacles in Edinburgh, would enjoy perpetuating the old
tradition of play acting, or reviving it in his pleasure garden. The
'timber hous' *may* have been a proper theatre at the centre of the
garden and it may have been covered with canvas, painted to resemble
stone. We know that the great wooden public theatres (and wooden
banqueting houses) were covered with canvas 'painted all the outsides
of the same most artificiallie, with a worke called rustike, much like to
stone'. Frances Yates refers to similar treatment as one of the expensive
improvements made in the second Globe Theatre, funded by James I:

> The use of the rustication with battlements and bay window
> gives an extraordinary hybrid effect to the whole, but shows …
> that the illusion aimed at was that of a great modern mansion,
> which yet could be easily switched to present the sterner
> aspect of fortified castle or town.

Plants had previously been valued for their use in herbal medicine, but
John Parkinson in *Paradisi in Sole* encouraged people to enjoy the
beauty of the new arrivals. New plants were also collectors' items, many
of them valuable. By the middle of the seventeenth century, the
legendary Tradescants, father and son, were able to list an impressive
range of the plants on offer to dedicated collectors. Among the
Tradescants' purchases were 'gilliflowers' and 'fortye fritelaries' from
Leiden at 3d each and 800 Haarlem tulips for 10s per hundred.
Cherries, medlars, quince, roses, Russian and North African species, as
well as trees, shrubs and perennials, obtained through the Virginia
Company in North America, burgeoned in the Tradescants' London
garden, which was probably also a nursery. Up and down the land,
individuals now grew plants for pleasure and obtained them through
private exchange or from the nurseries springing up to sell them.

Everyone had their favourites. John Reid loved carnations,
cranesbills and tulips, James Sutherland relished a particular Scottish
rose, and James Justice, who leaps on to the eighteenth-century
theatrum botanicum stage, was described as a 'tulip-maniac' but he was
also a plantsman who relished the cultivation of auriculas and other
tender plants. Vegetable seeds were in demand too. Seed lists from 1681
found at Cawdor Castle demonstrate that the thanes were keen to

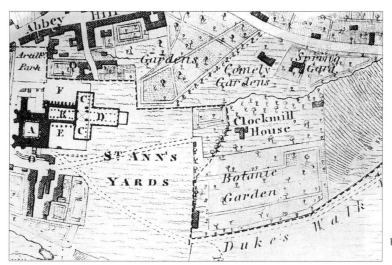

The site of the first botanic or physic garden beside the Duke's Walk at Holyrood Park.

introduce new varieties. British horticulturalists, gardeners and botanists, royal patrons, rich merchants and churchmen took up the mania for plant collecting from the increasingly rich trove of plant stock that continued to energise the study of medicine and the development of botany as a science and led to the development of the physic gardens.

The Edinburgh physic garden, nestled under Arthur's Seat near Holyrood Palace, was at first a cross between the two. It had been founded by two doctors, Andrew Balfour (1630–94) and Robert Sibbald (1641–1715), who had both studied medicine on the Continent and followed the European practice of cultivating medicinal herbs in the garden as a way of introducing the study of botany. But the practise lagged 'woefully behind' in Scottish medical schools, so Sibbald leased a piece of land in order to introduce the study and cultivation of medicinal herbs to the curriculum. Balfour and Sibbald, eminent scientists, botanists and natural historians, were both knighted in 1682 for their contributions to science and society. Balfour's library of over 3000 volumes and his collection of scientific artefacts were said to be among the finest of the kingdom. Sibbald produced *Scotia Illustra* (1684) for Charles II – an account of Scottish geography, archeology and native flora. He corresponded with John Beaton, also an outstanding historian, genealogist and folklorist of the west coast medical kindred. Here was 'an interesting juxtaposition of the old and

the new', as John Bannerman says, 'for Sibbald was the first professor of medicine at Edinburgh University'. Many of the plants in *Scotia Illustrata* appeared in the catalogue of plants in the physic garden, *Hortus Medicus Edinburgensis* (1683), drawn up by James Sutherland, its first Regius Keeper.

As the architect for Holyrood Palace, Sir William Bruce must have been fascinated by the developing physic garden at St Anne's Yard, just beyond the palace walls. From its conception here in 1670, the garden – about the size of a tennis court – had been linked with the palace garden. Sitting half a mile away in the Dunbar's Close Garden, if I close my eyes, I can almost smell the soft sweet Scottish rose so beloved by the first curator of the Edinburgh physic garden. 'A Scottish rose with most fragrant white flowers' was included among native plants 'ordinarily cultivated in the fields' which James Sutherland swept into the gardens he tended.

He took his responsibilities as keeper of Edinburgh's physic gardens and overseer of Holyrood House garden seriously, making 'many painful journeys in all the Seasons of the year, to recover what the Kingdom produceth of Variety', as he recorded in his notebook. It would not be surprising if these journeys included visits to the herbal gardens of the Beatons in the Gaelic-speaking world with whom he corresponded. The wildflowers he collected, 'ordinarily cultivated in the fields', samples of the native flora of Scotland as well as escapees from the gardens of monastic orders and the nobility, included hemlock, hawkweed, lesser celandine and a range of poppies. The initial stock of the Edinburgh garden had been based on a collection of around 1000 plants donated by a young aristocrat with a passion for travel and natural history, Patrick Murray, Laird of Livingston. Sutherland needed a great deal of plant stock, for in addition to tending the first physic gardens, he was overseer of The Palace of Holyroodhouse garden, and in 1675 a second garden, about an acre in extent, was leased on the site of the present Waverley Station.

By 1683 this Trinity Hospital garden contained 2000 plants: herbs, vegetables and flowers. In the palace garden, Sutherland grew a similar range but he also introduced 'fine exetick forraign plants' there, including melons and citrus fruits whose cultivation must have involved heated greenhouses. He corresponded with key botanists and

The founder of the physic garden, Dr Andrew Sibbald, produced *Scotia Illustrata* (1684), an account of Scottish geography, archeology and native flora, for Charles II. The plant on the right of the plate, *Sibbaldia procumbens*, was named after him.

© Royal Botanic Garden, Edinburgh.

horticulturists abroad and was the recipient of interesting seed and plant catalogues. One of his correspondents was John Reid in New Jersey, who wrote in a letter to a friend:

> There are a great store of Garden herbs here. I have not had time to inquire into them all, neither to send some of the many pleasant, (tho' to me unknown) plants of this country, to James Sutherland, physick Gardener at Edinburgh, but tell him, I will not forget him, when opportunity offers.

Indeed, Reid had referred to Sutherland in *The Scots Gard'ner* – in a symbiotic marketing exercise, the book was on sale at the physic garden – 'If you would be further satisfied in the varieties of plants, consult the Learned and most Ingenious Mr James Sutherland's Catalogue Physick Gardener at Edinburgh.'

Sutherland classified his plants as 'natives' or as 'useful in medicine' or as 'annuals'; and he divided the garden into a section containing 'simples' arranged alphabetically for the beginner to study and into another area where plants were arranged and classified according to the 'latest Authors of Botanie' and in particular his 'incomparable Countreyman Doctor Morison'. Robert Morison, an Aberdonian, was one of the great horticulturists of the age, renowned as superintendent of the Duke of Orleans' garden at Blois. In 1660 he had become Charles II's physician and, after his appointment as professor of Botany at Oxford University, he developed close links with the Oxford physic garden. Morison knew a lot about the characteristics of 'forraign' plants and how to handle them and no doubt gave James Sutherland and other Scots gardeners good advice about their cultivation in the variety of climates and soils to be found north of the Border. He obtained many new foreign plants for the Oxford and Edinburgh gardens.

Eventually, basil, cistus, sea holly, lilies, hollyhocks, lavender, camomile and tarragon grew beside wild things such as bindweed, harebells and cranesbills in Sutherland's gardens. Everything had its place. Some introductions we can only wonder at: 'the deadly carrot', 'flesh coloured Flower of Constantinople', 'the Sensitive Plant' and 'Great hairy codded Willow-herbe'. Catalogued trees included larch, beech, holly, lime, yew and horse chestnut. The diligent keeper used 'all Care and Industry by forraign Correspondence to Acquire both Seeds and Plants from the Levant, Italy, Spain, France, Holland, England [and the] east and west Indies'. After all, his stated aim in the introduction to *A Catalogue of the Plants in the Physical Garden at Edinburgh* or *Hortus Medicus Edinburgensis* (1683) was to encourage the 'Interchange of Plants, which they can spare and I want, with others which They want and I can spare'. Indeed by the time he retired, on the eve of Union in 1706, he was able to claim that the plant stock that had passed through his green fingers compared well with gardens abroad 'for Number and Rarity of Plants'.

Imaginative garden design transformed and redefined itself in the Baroque revival when the enclosed worlds of the *hortus conclusus* and the artful pleasaunce could be opened up to take in the wider landscape beyond the garden walls, with vistas, allees and reference points for the eye: obelisks, statuary, topiary, lakes, summerhouses and follies. Sir William Bruce (Balcaskie and Kinross), William Adam (Hopetoun, Arniston, Mavisbank and Penicuik House) and John Erskine, 11th Earl of Mar (Alloa), represent the architects and gentlemen-architects who designed the house in the landscape. Though plans for many of these schemes exist – here we are on firmer ground with far more documentary evidence to describe design and horticulture – imagination is still required to reinvent them. To some extent, after the Union of the Crowns, English garden design began to influence Scottish schemes. The court and its associates in London were, after all, busy anglifying themselves and their numbers swelled inordinately after the Parliamentary Union of 1707, after which British garden historians like to include Scotland and to mention the 'army' of Scots gardeners that crossed the Border to seek work.

Glasgow is an interval, a time to take stock, a visit to a childhood friend who has appreciated my enthusiasm for the pleasaunce at Edzell. My reflection stares back at me, puzzled, on the polished surface of the windows of a Glasgow bookstore. Stars, planetary deities, Grammatica, Musica, Charity, Fortitude and the ubiquitous number seven still tease my mind, but I must move on. Double-decker buses bound for

Kelvingrove or Garscadden, taxis, cars, scooters, pedestrians flash across the plate glass window. There is not much time, I think glumly. The publisher's deadline seems perilously close and there remains a century of landscapes to travel. It's time to move on to Fife where Sir William Bruce's masterpieces, Balcaskie and Kinross, beckon.

In the harbour town of St Monans I discover, west of the half-circle of its womb-like harbour, long-fingered gardens behind couthy, pantiled, crow-stepped buildings, their lineaments dating back at least to the seventeenth century: lands or rigs, some of them still planted vigorously with herbs, plants and vegetables. At the east end of town grander merchants' houses, free-standing, have long since lost their garden landscapes, though some of today's owners have imaginatively reconstructed what suits them: a patio for roses, mallow, pansies and honeysuckle, a terraced garden you have to climb steeply up to until you look over the mansion's pantiled roof to the sea, rather as you do at Culross Palace.

The crowstep gable of the house with the outside stair where I'm staying in a sheltered, traffic-free courtyard dates back to the fifteenth century and the title deeds determine that here was once the village wash house, communal, as were the baking ovens and the services of the blacksmith. The sheltered garden was once much larger, the drying or bleaching green for the families living round about. In the morning I rake the gravel of the Japanese-style garden. There is no grass; only silver gravel and large stones, judiciously placed. This is the imaginative landscape the owner has chosen as suitable for a twenty-first-century *hortus conclusus* whose starkness reflects the sea. Later, I linger in the churchyard beside lichen-encrusted sixteenth- and seventeenth-century headstones, some embellished with mementi mori, skull and crossbones, the hour glass, the tools of the deceased's trade: hammer, baking paddles or ship's oars. The church of St Monans is Norman, with a pyramidical spire. Every town on the coast here has one. Beacons for ships at sea. Remember, remember. *Aides-mémoire.*

St Monans' exciting triumvirate – church, doocot and castle – draw me on, up a wonky path edged with wildflowers: valerian and yellow wallflower, woven like a scented garland round the crest of the doocot where pigeons still fly in and out and breed. No one eats the birds now, but once they supplied valuable winter meat particularly to the inhabitants of Newark House, a small castle, almost infinitely ruined, where I now sit, mulling over what I've discovered so far about gardens and the art of memory.

The afternoon is soft and warm; that ineffable mixed scent of sea and earth hangs on the breeze. The sea is calm; the Bass Rock, the Isle of May, Whalebone Law are gigantic natural sculptures in the distance. Images for the art of memory of a different kind – my memory of a midsummer spell at St Monans, the nearest town to Balcaskie where Sir William Bruce, in the middle of the seventeenth century, constructed the main axial path of his garden to take in a view of the Bass Rock to the south-west and north-west to Kellie Law.

As I have discovered, Fife had been well supplied with 'gentimenis places and gret palices' since the Renaissance and the families who inhabited them were socially linked entrepreneurs and employers. Some of them were royalists like William Bruce and his neighbour Alexander, 3rd Earl of Kellie, at Kellie Castle near Pittenweem. Kellie fought with Charles II during the Civil War at the Battle of Worcester in 1651 and, after brief imprisonment in the Tower of London, exiled himself in Holland before returning to Kellie Castle in 1661. It has been suggested that Cromwellian rule had the effect of sending some landowners into enforced exile on their estates where they concentrated on improving their land. Certainly, the Civil War influenced the nature of design both in the house and grounds.

Little is known about the early garden at Kellie Castle, whose present garden, redesigned in the twentieth century to some extent by Robert Lorimer (whose feeling for historical sources also guided his reconstruction of the garden at Earlshall near St Andrews), is one of the loveliest in Scotland. But the hand of Bruce can be detected in the house. The 'noble symmetry' of its heraldically decorated plaster ceiling (1676) was made, designed and probably carried out under the supervision of Bruce, who was at the time rehabilitating and adding to the Palace of Holyroodhouse for Charles II. Some of the most skilled plasterers of the age, including George Dunstanfield, worked at Holyrood and the late Christopher Hussey suggested that Bruce may have sent assistant plasterers over to Fife, 'bringing their templates with them' to work at Balcaskie and Kellie alongside local craftsmen.

Embellished plaster ceilings were in favour now; painted ceilings were regarded as old-fashioned. Three ceilings at Kellie Castle are dated 1676 and the stunning Vine Room ceiling (Lorimer copied it for a bedroom at twentieth-century Ardkinglas, Loch Fyne) is dated to the early 1680s. Bruce's influence is at work too in the roundel painting depicting Mount Olympus as if seen through an opening in the sky, by De Witt who was employed by the architect at Holyroodhouse. Indeed, the artist had been 'called from his owne countrey [Holland]' by Sir William in 1673 and had been paid £120 in 1675 'for ane piece of historie paynted and placed on the roofe of the King's bed chamber … on the syde towards the privie garden' at Holyrood.

Bearing in mind the new emphasis on house and garden ground as an entity, the two neighbours and friends, Bruce and Kellie, must have improved the garden at Kellie Castle. Although 'land-girt' (without the direct sea views that inspired Bruce's imaginative leap at Balcaskie, where the distant view became an integral aspect of the design), it is likely to have retained the traditional triumvirate of the Scottish walled garden: formal garden, orchard and vegetable and herb garden, surrounded by stout walls to protect the garden's rather exposed situation.

The Civil War offered an interregnum to Royalist landowners. Here was a time for thought and action in one's own earthly paradise. New ideas about architecture and garden landscape energised the intelligentsia even as most tinkered with tradition.

At Pitmedden in Aberdeenshire Sir Alexander Seton, the first baronet, levelled his garden ground and maintained its intricate box-edged parterres by 1675, following a grand but traditional approach. Seton was another Royalist and another friend of Sir William Bruce, whose radical ideas about designed landscapes had been demonstrated at Balcaskie a decade earlier. He had already altered his towerhouse home by 1665 into what he called 'the first mansion house in Scotland', where the hanging terraces sweep from the broad parterres down to the parkland. From the garden terrace an axial path shoots like an arrow in the direction of the Bass Rock on the other side of the Firth of Forth. The gannet-infested rock became a feature of the design of the garden at Balcaskie. Bruce led the eye of the beholder beyond the terrace, beyond the garden and the parkland, over the sea, into another world.

After creating that small masterpiece he wanted to move on himself, to the challenge of a new house, at Kinross, where he took two years to design and lay out the garden and parkland before the house in the classical style was built. Bruce understood that soon the 'guid and greit' of Scotland would no longer aspire to live in towerhouses but in temples. The classical style he had studied in English buildings during his frequent visits there would soon creep over the Border.

Before he took on Kinross, Bruce lent a hand at Pittmedden Great Garden, whose owner Alexander Seton, a distinguished advocate, was knighted like Bruce by Charles II in 1664. Bruce and Seton were men who stood out among relatively few in an underpopulated country. Bruce often travelled to the Continent, ostensibly for business but also to carry messages to and from Charles II, exiled in France. On an outing from Paris he visited the chateau of Vaux-le-Vicomte whose architect was Le Vau and whose large formal gardens were among the masterpieces of Le Nôtre, the winning team later engaged by Louis XIV at Versailles. The house and garden Bruce would create at Kinross towards the end of the century reveal his admiration for both Le Vau and Le Nôtre and he shared his enthusiasm and knowledge of Vaux-le-Vicomte, as well as other Continental landscape masterpieces, with Scottish comrades such as Seton, and probably the Earl of Morton at Aberdour Castle.

Alexander Seton began his garden on land sloping to the east, excavated to be on a lower level than the western ground. His Great Garden at Pitmedden would be a 'marvelous amalgam of parterres, buttresses, herbacous borders, grass and fruit trees protected by high and staunch granite walls'. Parterre design was a particularly ingenious way of writing the family motto large-scale on the landscape. He divided the lower garden into four parterres outlined by box hedges and divided by turf paths. The intricate designs of his parterres must be seen or 'read' from above; thus he had viewing terraces constructed on the high retaining wall of the garden which divided the upper and lower garden ground with identical pavilions at either end. In the centre of the wall twin stairs led down from the upper garden where there was a fountain and a recessed font. One of the pavilions retains its original appearance today: a two-storey building with a rib-vaulted lower floor and summerhouse apartment upstairs, complete with a

fireplace. The pavilion recalls the summerhouse at Edzell and anticipates the pavilions at Kinross in the ogival outline of its roof.

Although Sir John Clerk of Penicuik was born a year after Pitmedden was laid out, and started to write *A Countryman's Diary* forty years later (1726), his words seem to mirror the intentions of Alexander Seton and other pre-Union landscapers:

> Around the Fabrick spread the wide Parterre
> Like to a verdant Mantle edgd with Gold
> Or an embroyderd Carpet all perfumd
> With Indian Sweets, here with a mystick mien
> Let Nature in the Pride of blooming Flowrs
> Triumphant sit, and all the Gardiners Toils
> Direct with matchless grace.

Near-contemporary sources inspired the National Trust for Scotland's twentieth-century reconstruction of the parterres of the Great Garden of Pitmedden. Three parterre designs were copied from Gordon of Rothiemay's drawings of the garden of the Palace of Holyroodhouse with the legends *Tempus Fugit* and a central sundial of twenty-four facets. The fourth parterre depicts the Saltire and thistle with Seton's coat of arms (three crescents and a bleeding heart) and the mottoes *Susteno Sanguine Signa* ('with blood I bear the standard') and *Merces*

Parterres in the lower garden at Pitmedden.

Haec Certa Laborum ('this sure reward of our labours'). The parterre refers to the death of the Alexander Seton's father John in the service of Charles I at the Battle of Brig O' Dee (1639).

Other influences on Seton's garden derived from the gardens of the 'seats' or chateaux in the Edinburgh area, and the gardens at the Palace of Holyroodhouse rebuilt by Sir William Bruce for Charles II in 1671, a year after James Sutherland became superintendent of the physic garden near the palace. Seton is likely to have called in on Bruce at both of those gardens on his frequent trips to Edinburgh in one or other of his capacities. Lord Pitmedden was a Senator of the College of Justice and a Baronet of Nova Scotia (1683), and represented Aberdeenshire in the Scottish Parliament. Apart from its architectural outlines, the original Pitmedden garden has long since disappeared and so has the house. The scholarly reconstruction of the garden has been laid out beside the nineteenth-century house with the recent addition of a herb garden.

Sir William Bruce had a lot on his mind, including gardens, when he rode away from Balcaskie in 1683, the same year as his friend, Seton, was made a baronet. He left behind Lady Bruce, who must wait patiently until her husband would be ready to receive her at Kinross House, a decade later.

After 1660 a great flowering of confidence had mirrored the taste for extravagant display on the one hand and an authoritarian need to control and subjugate nature on the other. The highly formalised French gardens and their designed landscapes, which Bruce knew at first hand, would influence the design of Kinross. It would be a considerable masterpiece. Under the Baroque influence of late seventeenth-century Europe, Scottish walled gardens were becoming sophisticated, and took a strong architectural lead from the house. Often both house and garden were designed by the same person, who also displayed his hand in the design of walls, terraces, summerhouses and other features.

The garden Sir William created at Kinross bridged the Baroque and the classical; its design obeyed the dictum of John Reid in *The Scots Gard'ner* that all walks, trees and hedges must radiate from the house 'like the sun sending forth its beams'. But an important new component revolutionised the design. Symmetrically formal, enclosed gardens now became bonded with the natural world beyond the walls

through the inspired use of geometrical devices and focal points on a grander scale than Balcaskie. At Kinross, carefully positioned axis paths, terracing, fountains, sundials, statuary and the like had the effect of guiding the eye outwards to draw in the surrounding countryside. And, from time to time, members of the family and their friends might even be enticed to slip away from the ordered world of the house, through gates that gave direct access to woods, rivers, grazing lands or whatever lay beyond the garden walls. Beyond the walls the garden's atmosphere of contained and considered formality gives way to wildness and wet. Here the wanderer is under the spell of the castle on the loch; here an adventure might begin on however small a scale.

Sir William had purchased the Kinross estate from the Earl of Morton, whose forebears had controlled Loch Leven Castle and guarded Mary, Queen of Scots, during her imprisonment there. At Kinross, too, he would link the garden with the natural world beyond by providing an axial view of the romantic Loch Leven Castle, which resembled a ruined folly when seen from the formal terraces of the house. To the 'fervent Royalist', though, the castle meant more than an architectural feature of his designed landscape. It was also an emotive *aide-mémoire* encouraging thoughts of the tragic young Queen: a memorial.

The same year as James Sutherland and his physic garden moved to the Trinity Hospital site work began on the designed landscape at Kinross. Sutherland, Bruce and Morton – an intriguing trio, linked by a love of gardening. The Morton papers refer to gardening at Aberdour from the 1650s and to the fact that James Sutherland delivered plants there in the 1690s. Lord Morton's neighbour at Donibristle, Lord Moray, had been similarly involved in horticulture a few decades earlier and at his other properties, Canongate House and Darnaway Castle, as headings from the Darnaway papers reveal:

Accounts for making the garden at Donibristle, 1639
Accounts to gardener for watges, trees, flowers, for garden, Donibristle, 1646
Plants in garden, Donibristle, 1655.

Top.
Kinross House.

Bottom.
Kinross: The main axial path leads the beholder's eye to the Fish Gate and beyond, to Loch Leven and its castle.

Both © Sheila Mackay, 2001.

Sutherland and Bruce must have exchanged plants, too. After all, the stated aim of Sutherland's 1683 catalogue had been to encourage the 'Interchange of Plants'.

Bruce's elegant design set Kinross House at the centre of a rectangular garden enclosed by four walls, with a separate kitchen garden and orchard. Twelve square areas were designated as parterres on the architect's original design, but only four, in front of the house, are depicted with the ornate plantings of heraldic designs and patterns that were characteristic of Renaissance gardens such as Pittmedden. Considerable sums were spent on plantings. Seedlings were imported from England and Holland as well as a large number of fir and oak trees. Bruce's son, John, sent a box of plants from Paris in 1681 which included around 300 horse chestnut seedlings.

The new house was almost ready to receive Lady Bruce after Thomas Back, a mason, built the garden and orchard walls in 1693, the same year as John Hamilton constructed the sundial and James Anderson built the attractive ogee summerhouses. Two Dutch stonemasons, Peter Paul Boyse and Cornelius van Nerven, sculpted naked boys riding dolphins and cornucopias of fruit to snake along the stone arches of the magnificent Fish Gate. Through these gates there is direct access to the woods, lake and lands beyond the garden walls.

The new garden at Kinross was well protected from biting winds by extensive plantations and shelterbelts on either side of the entrance driveway as well as by high garden walls. The climate at Kinross is typical of central Scotland, where gardens are exposed to the easterly winds blowing across the loch. From the house itself, panoramic views draw the eye eastwards across Loch Leven to the Lomond Hills and south towards Benartie Hill. Views to Castle Island and westward to Glendevon Forest, the town of Kinross and the Ochil Hills form part of the strong axis running east–west through the centre of the house. Little has altered of Bruce's plan as I stand enchanted in the garden on a warm and cloudless early autumn day. All along the edge of a herbaceous border red admiral butterflies flicker beside fat bees on pads of purpling sedum, and larkspurs and delphiniums shed seeds from crusty pods. The afternoon sun is low in the sky behind smoke from the gardener's bonfire. Here are topiary, statuary, box hedging, sundials and axial paths leading to the summerhouses. One of

Kinross: Detail of a sculpted naked boy riding a dolphin from the Fish Gate.

© Sheila Mackay, 2001.

145

the family, or perhaps a family friend, smocked and sunhatted, oil-paints a landscape, a view of a corner of the rose garden and its ogival entrance. Several gardeners are at work, unobtrusively raking and clipping. The newly mown grass scents the air with very heaven. Here is a tranquil theatre, generously open to public viewing by the present owner, where two *lions guardant* peep over the topiary and Atlas raises the world on his shoulders. A graceful fountain, recently added, dances above waterlilies in the pond. The herbaceous borders must be far more floribundant than in Bruce's time: luxuriant annuals and perennials on well-manured soil, from the humble blue Michaelmas daisy to riotous roses, hipping now as they approach the last months of the year. And herbs, presumably formerly contained in neat knots, run rampant among the fading flowers: marjoram, thyme, sage and lavender. Trees emphasise the east–west axis parallel to the house and Sir William's son John's chestnuts, fully mature and spreading, punctuate the lower garden.

During the latter part of his life, Sir William was imprisoned at least three times for his support of the Royalist cause and at the turn of the century, ten years before he died, he gave Kinross to John. A few years later Daniel Defoe recorded his impressions of Kinross in *A Tour Through the Whole Island of Great Britain*: 'At the West End of the Lake (the Gardens reaching down to the very Water's edge) stands the most beautiful and regular Piece of Architecture in all Scotland.'

James Sutherland retired in 1706. He is still remembered as the man who put the Royal Botanic Garden of Edinburgh on the map. The genus *Sutherlandia*, a group of South African shrubs belonging to the pea family (*Leguminosae*), is named after him. Sutherland's contemporary, John Evelyn, had meantime been studying the development of gardening styles in Europe. This knowledge, combined with his recommendations on the use and growth of trees and shrubs, would contribute to the emergence of the English landscape style of the eighteenth century, which only the seriously rich could afford to take up in Scotland. The English landscape garden movement is held to have its roots in the concept of *sharawadgi*, first used by Sir William Temple in his essay *Upon the Gardens of Epicurus* (1692). *Sharawadgi* refers to the spirit of the perfect garden according to the Chinese method of planting in an informal, free style that would be adopted by

Kinross: Detail of sculpted loaves, fishes and cornucopias above the Fish Gate.

© Sheila Mackay, 2001.

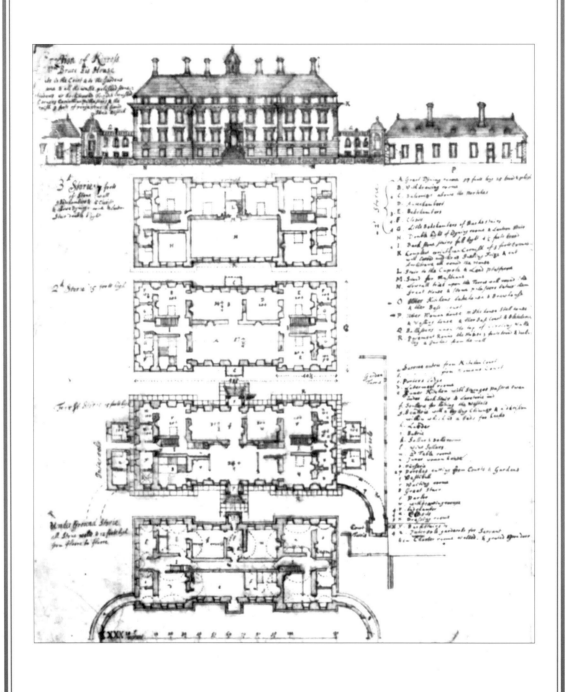

landscape designers in the eighteenth century when there emerged a craze for chinoiserie in the home as well as the garden.

For want of cash or lack of imagination, or from love of plain sense and no nonsense, and frequently elements of all these factors, many landowning gentry of the late seventeenth century continued to improve in a traditional, unsensational style. North-east of Corstorphine Hill Sir John Foulis, Clerk of Sasines, springs vividly to life on his Ravelston estate, thanks to his meticulous records that reflect the gardening and estate management undertaken by a couthy Scots landowner at the end of the century. In 1681, for example, he ordered 'rosamundies', red and white-striped roses still unusual in Britain. He grew pears, apples, cherries, plums, apricots, peaches, strawberries, redcurrants, raspberries and vegetables in such abundance that he could sell the excess to the markets of Edinburgh. His social engagements included discussions, card-playing, the theatre, the races, golf at Leith and Bruntsfield, bowls and visiting other estates. What had been learned at Ravelston – he had limed the fields, repaired fences and buildings to house his cows, sheep and pigs, he had planted trees, stocked the gardens with fruit trees, vegetables and flowers – translated to a new estate Sir John went on to lay out at Woodhall, Juniper Green. On Christmas Day in 1700 the gardener stepped into the kitchen of his enlightened employer to make the celebratory meal of 'beife, mutton, rabets fouls breed the 12 bottles claret 4 bottles seck all for £2.18. 0d. Scots'.

Sir John's Woodhall records describe kitchen garden stock obtained from a seed merchant called 'Ha ferguson': 'leek, onion, beetrave, orange caret, silesia lettuce, colifour, radish, purseline, indian cress, suger peas, dutch asparagus, apricock, and 40 young firrs'. In 1705 he started the major works of enclosing the land and rebuilding walls: 'the masons began this morning to the highing the north dyke of the wester orchard and ended the bankdyke yesternight. the 2 mawers began to maw the intak [enclosed land] this morning.' He paid the masons and barrowmen for 'work at the dykes, lyme, and a day at the hedges in the park', for 'biging highting, kaiping and casting dyks', and gave one of them a discount of '13 peckes of meall'. The thirst-inducing nature of the men's work is sometimes recognised in additional 'drink monie'.

Plan drawing of Kinross House and gardens attributed to Alexander Edward.

© The Royal Commission on the Ancient and Historical Monuments of Scotland.

Meanwhile, the Ravelston estate, too, was developing under Sir John's aegis:

> I have agreed wt the gardiner at raevelstoune for the yards doucat and ridwalk [doocot and raised pathway through the garden] … and what muck [manure] I shall make, besyde the muck the tennent is toe have of the strae [straw] I am to have libertie upon publick occasions of passage of the ridwalk. He is to prune and prin up the wall trees. He is not to meddle wt the gardein.

When I slip through the wrought-iron gates into the secret garden at Dunbar's Close, I leave behind the noise and bustle of the Royal Mile, its open-topped tourist buses and squawking gulls, its centuries of Scottish history soon to be expanded into a new phase enshrined in the twenty-first-century Scottish Parliament building, a quarter of a mile away. This late afternoon in high summer I sense a peculiar poignancy as I sit as if in a time capsule on the stone bench beyond the espaliered apple trees. The garden is a seventeenth-century reconstruction in the deep canyon of the Canongate below Calton Hill where the sun strikes Thomas Hamilton's neo-classical Royal High School. The 1707 Union is round the corner; so is neo-classicism. The 'glorious Revolution' of 1688–9 had put William and Mary on the English throne and re-established Presbyterianism. Although Lowland Scotland had little liking of the Highland tribes, its population had been shocked by the King's connivance in the murder of the MacDonalds of Glencoe in 1692 and, two years later, in the slaughter of 'the popish clan' Clanranald on Eigg. The Jacobite, Graham of Claverhouse, had been killed at Killiecrankie in 1689 and religious schisms tore at the fabric of society. But even these events had been overshadowed by the betrayal of Scots settlers in the Darien Peninsula and the heavy loss of investment in the scheme to establish a Scots trading colony there in 1698. The Alien Act of 1705 further fuelled Scots outrage – Scots were to be regarded as aliens in England – and effectively halted trading between England and Scotland.

Against a background of unrest and violence in the capital, the Articles of Union were prepared by the Scottish Parliament. The

Top.
Dunbar's Close: espaliered apple trees underplanted with thrift and lavender beds.

Bottom.
Dunbar's Close: central bay trees in thyme-filled knots.

Both © Sheila Mackay, 2001.

Opposite.
The hermit's cave at
the Hermitage was on
the eighteenth-century
tourist trail.

Right.
Dunbar's Close:
view from the
seventeenth-century
garden to the eighteenth-
century neo-classical Old
High School by Thomas
Hamilton.

Both © Sheila Mackay, 2001.

152

anguish of Scotland, the shotgun bride, labelled neither Scottish nor British, set her descendants' teeth on edge and Scots became ashamed to use their native tongue. After Union, trade, cultural and political links with England opened up; elocution lessons became the vogue, even David Hume and Adam Ferguson anglicised their speech; and an unprecedented demand erupted for classical-style homes and gardens from newly wealthy and titled Union supporters, anxious to show outwardly their new sense of self-esteem.

CHAPTER 9

'Furor Hortensis'

THE DARLING COUNTRY SEAT MUST ONLY BE

WHERE GOOD AND BOUNTEOUS NATURE SEEMS INCLIN'D

BY MODERATE CULTURE TO REWARD OUR PAINS

Acute national poverty preceded the devastating year of 1709 when much of Scotland was scourged by famine. This double disaster did not prevent certain families, who emerged powerful and wealthy after the Union, from landscaping their estates on a grand scale in emulation of the best designs in Europe. Only the seriously rich could plant broad plantations and pleasure gardens, as at Dalkeith, Drumlanrig, Hopetoun, Blair, Taymouth, Yester and Inveraray, one of the most ambitious designed landscapes of the period. In the eighteenth century, although estate gardening and landscaping began to be well documented, imaginative leaps are still required to recreate original intentions from maps and written descriptions of the time. Detailed maps were becoming available. In 1750 James Dorret, who was employed by the Duke of Argyll, produced the first good outline of Scotland in a general map showing the shires, forts and roads. The Dorret map was soon followed by the 'Roy Map', the celebrated Military Survey of Scotland, 1747–55. The survey had been commissioned after the Forty-Five, when it was discovered that no reliable maps of the Highlands existed; it was completed under the direction of General William Roy, and showed in great detail estates, gardens, woods and shelterbelts:

> The courses of all the Rivers and numerous streams were followed to the source, and measured; all the Roads, and the many Lakes of salt-water and fresh were surveyed, as well as such other intermediate places and cross lines as were found necessary for filling up the country.

The Scottish lion 'couchant guardant' (crouching and watching) after Union. Plasterwork by Joseph Enzer (1742–3), House of Dun, Montrose.

Reprinted by permission of the National Trust for Scotland.

Four plans exist to demonstrate the development of the designed landscape at Inveraray Castle for Archibald, Duke of Argyll (1682–1761), who was renowned as a great plantsman and forester. After the estate had first been laid out in the middle of the sixteenth century, it was extensively altered in the 1720s, completely redesigned by 1756 and, again, in the picturesque style, at the end of the century. Entire estates were reconstructed by professional architects and landscape designers such as the Adam family, William Boutcher, Thomas Winter, Roger Morris and Robert Mylne. Impressive formal allees appeared, punctuated by vistas, follies and obelisks. Vast

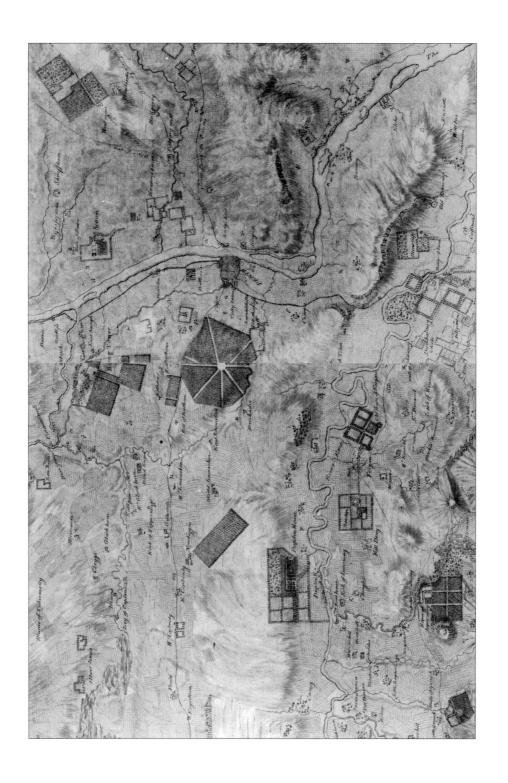

parterres and flower gardens were created round new or improved mansions or palaces on a previously unknown scale and in imitation of the English formal style, which in turn reflected French, Italian and Dutch designs. Formal gardens (fully illustrated in books of the period, as stereotypical and easy to copy as they had been a century earlier) lay at the centre of the overall design which opened out into woods and parkland. There was a growing tendency to divide the garden ground into compartments, each with a different character, and the plant stock was more colourful and extravagant than ever before.

John Macky in 1714 wrote of Yester:

> The parterre and garden behind the house is very spacious and fine. There is a handsome basin with *jet d'eaux* in the middle of the parterre, with four good statues upon pedestals in each corner. There is an abundance of evergreens, and green slopes regularly dispos'd; and to the west on an artificial mound is a pleasant summerhouse.

Accounts from 1708 refer to work on the pond, garden gates, summerhouse, bridges and grotto. Macky wrote of the parklands:

Above.

'Landskip' showing Taymouth Castle and grounds by Loch Tay, attributed to James Norie and John Griffier, around 1733 and 1739.

© The Scottish National Portrait Gallery, reproduced by permission.

Opposite.

View of the city of Perth, the River Tay, roads, farms, estates, buildings and other features in the surrounding countryside from the Military Survey (1747–55), or 'Roy Map'.

Mat C.9.B Sheet 17 Section 7/2 and 7/3; by permission of The British Library.

A Parterre after ye English manner

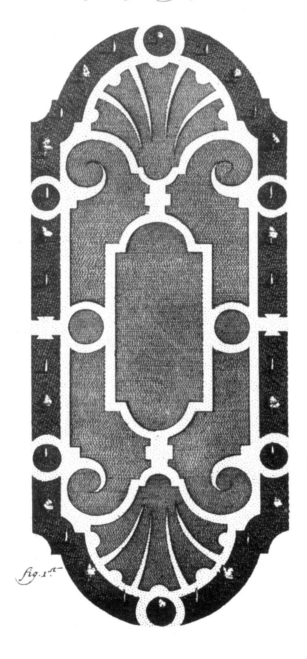

fig. 1.a

the best planted park I ever saw: the park walls are about eight miles in circumference: and I dare venture to say, there is a full million of full grown trees in it. In short it is larger, as well walled, and more regularly planted than Richmond in Surrey.

In *Britannia Illustrata*, published between 1707 and 1715, Johannes Kip and Leonard Knyff showed engravings of English estates in the French tradition with long avenues, parterres, and clipped and regimented trees and flowers. But by 1728 Batty Langley and others had adopted a radically new approach. There was nothing more shocking than a stiff regular garden, they declared, and Langley decried gardens that are 'fluffed up with trifling flower Knots, parterres of Cut-work, Embroidery, Wildernesses of Ever-Greens and sometimes of Forest Trees'. *Irregularity* became the new buzz word in the English horticultural world. Serpentine, meandering paths were in, and wildernesses were no longer to be planted like orchards 'but in a rural manner, as if they had receiv'd their situation from nature itself'.

In many parts of Scotland, of course, there was no need to contrive wilderness, though later in the century, as Lord Kames advocated, such areas might be tamed. Received wisdom filtered up from the English formalists like Langley on trees 'that cause fine shade' which were not to be tortured by regimental clipping, though topiary

Opposite.
Parterre *à l'anglaise* after d'Argenville: an elegant pattern of cut turf and gravel walks.
John James, *The Theory and Practice of Gardening*, London (1712).

Reproduced by permission of the National Library of Scotland.

Top.
Batty Langley provided an alternative to French practice with designs introducing serpentine paths in *The New Principles of Gardening*, London (1728).

161

as *art* might be a different matter. Even as the parkland, formal gardens and walled gardens were being laid out at Inveraray, Yester, Hopetoun, Drumlanrig, Drummond and the other aristocratic estates, formal style was on the wane in England. This, however, did not deter some of the most favoured English garden designers of the day from designing formal landscapes in Scotland, whose cultivation they also supervised. Soil samples were sent to London from the Earl of Lauderdale's seat at Hatton, one of the most ambitious schemes of all. Hatton was designed by the foremost English garden advisers and nurserymen of the day, London and Wise, whose pupil, Stephen Switzer, would later recommend the 'irregularity' that had come into vogue in England.

Thomas, 6th Earl of Haddington (1680–1735), was quite taken by some elements of the landscape movement with its wildernesses and serpentine paths. 'Were I to plant a wilderness, there should be nothing in it but evergreens, flowering shrubs, trees that carry a fine blossom, and a kind of willow that hath a bark of bright yellow.' Wildernesses, he wrote,

> have not long been introduced to this country, and the way they were first laid out was, that they first pitched on a centre with straight views from it, terminating in as fine a prospect as could be had. Then, there were serpentine walks that run through the whole, hedged like the straight walks, and the angles planted with a variety of different trees; though now they are weary of the hedges.

His comments and use of the terms 'serpentine' and 'wilderness' (in the formal sense) suggest that Scottish landowners were well abreast of developments in the fast-changing world of English landscaping.

Hopetoun, with which Switzer was associated, fell to the great Scots architect, William Adam (1698–1748), who carried forward the pioneering approach of his predecessor, Sir William Bruce, who designed the landscape and house as a unity. Hopetoun would become one of the marvels of Scotland. Bruce had sited the earlier house at Hopetoun to face east with due regard for axial views. William Adam described Bruce's avenue as 'carrying your eye over two miles of the River Forth to the island and ruins of Inchgarvie and from thence forward along the River 22 miles or more to North Berwick Law'. That

view is interrupted by the two bridges over the Forth nowadays, but the designed landscape remains in outline much as William Adam planned it between 1720 and 1740. Following Scottish tradition, Adam divided the walled garden into three and he proposed to construct 'a canal … for Water Foull', an influence from the Dutch, in the largest section. In the second half of the century Hopetoun would be among the great estates where the landscape style promoted by followers of 'Capability' Brown was taken up.

Union supporters who were not members of the ruling aristocracy nevertheless required buildings to match the self-esteem bestowed by their new titles and wealth. Aspiring Scots quickly perceived the need to anglify themselves and to emulate the architectural style in vogue in the south: early Palladian. Each new house was unique yet obeyed certain precepts. Internally the central hall gave access to the apartments through one or more 'temple' porticoes. Externally the lower storey was rusticated at ground or basement level below the ashlar upper storey. Entry to the house was through the 'rustic' or directly into the hall behind the portico at the head of an external flight of steps. Great demand prompted a mini-building boom between 1730 and 1800. In the first part of the century William Adam, although called in to the very grandest projects, was a favoured architect of

In 1731 William Adam purchased the estate of Blair Cranbeth near Kinross and now called Blairadam. John Adam, his son, designed and laid out the 4-acre walled garden between 1755 and 1761. Many plant and fruit varieties as well as ancient larches, spruces and silver firs were sent to the Adam family by Duke Archibald of Inveraray, one of the great gardeners of the age.

Photograph © Nic Allen, with thanks to Keith Adam, supplied by the Royal Commission on the Ancient and Historical Monuments of Scotland.

clients desiring a classical country house and he was skilled, too, in landscape design. His practice flourished and, like Sir William Bruce before him, Adam made a point of touring the grand houses and grounds of England, marvels of the day, though often remote and isolated with difficult access, that were open for viewing.

In 1731 William Adam purchased the estate of Blair Cranbeth set in 'dull and uncompromising country' near Kinross, and supporting only one ash tree. By 1733 there was a simple house, built by William Adam to be his factor's residence and, by 1750, grounds laid out in the formal style. The subsequent evolution of 'The Blair', as the family called the estate, were recorded in *The Blair Adam Book* (1834) by the architect's grandson William with the encouragement of Sir Walter Scott. A series of numbered maps pinpoint three eras of development with the author's comments.

The house that William Adam built was a two-storey, five-bay mansion with a pedimented porch and he created a formal parkland with a series of avenues leading from the house. Some of the beech trees he planted remain. It was John Adam, his son, who designed and laid out the 4-acre walled garden between 1755 and 1761 with the Gardener's House and the Temple as well as the Coach-house and other estate houses. The heated double north wall of the garden was 18 feet high and 426 feet long. The Gardener's House was incorporated into the north wall at the head of a broad grass walk which bisected the garden on the north–south axis. The Temple was inserted into the east wall at the end of a broad gravel walk. Some fruit trees lining the inner walls remain though their age is uncertain. A nursery was started in 1750 to grow trees from seed and plans for peach and nectarine houses were drawn up.

Many plant and fruit varieties as well as ancient larches, spruces and silver firs were sent to the Adam family from Duke Archibald of Inveraray, one of the great gardeners of the age, who, stimulated by plant introductions and his passion to see how they would 'do' in British soil, set up an experimental garden and nursery on his estate at Whitton. The Scot, William Aiton (1731–93), curator of Kew Botanical Garden, published the *Hortus Kewensis* in 1780. The catalogue describes the plant collection at Kew and lists nearly every species under cultivation in England, including several important

introductions made by the Duke of Argyll: various andromedas, paper birch (*Betula papyrifera*) and poplar-leaved birch (*B. populifolia*), the hardy bonduc or Kentucky coffee tree (*Gymnocladus dioca*), Carolina or American holly (*Ilex opaca*), *Itea virginica*, and snowy mespilus or shadbush *(Amelanchier canadensis)*. Whitton was visited by outstanding horticulturalists and botanists of the day, including Aiton and Philip Miller (1691–1771), curator of the Chelsea Physic Garden, John Claudius Loudon and Peter Collinson, the eminent plant collector. The Duke received three boxes of wild seed from America imported by Peter Collinson. Horace Walpole noted the good results in his *Anecdotes on Planting in England*: 'The introduction of foreign trees and plants, which we owe principaly to Archibald, Duke of Argyll, contributed essentially to the richness of colouring so peculiar to our modern landscape.'

As the century progressed large numbers of English travellers came north to see developments in Scotland. Daniel Defoe had been sent to Edinburgh to report to the government on Scottish attitudes to the Act of Union and on trade potential. Books such as Defoe's *Tour Through the Whole Island of Great Britain*, Martin Martin's account of the Western Isles and Thomas Pennant's *Tour of Scotland* put the country on the map of cultivated ladies and gentlemen who enjoyed the *Ars Peregrinandi*; to visit the great homes of Scotland was to elevate the art. Defoe called Scotland the *terra incognita*. It is 'a country almost as little known to its southern brethren as Kamschatska [in Siberia]', wrote Pennant who visited Bruce's houses Kinross and Hopetoun: 'the handsomest [mansion] I saw in North Britain'. Defoe described 'pavilions and banqueting houses. ... and the greens trimm'd, spalier and hedges are in perfection' after viewing Drumlanrig in 1720. By 1740, plans for Drumlanrig's further improvement show the terraces cut out of the steep slope running down towards Marr Burn with a cascade flowing into a canal, all laid out by David Low, gardener to the 3rd Duke of Queensberry. In *A Journey through Scotland* (1732) John Macky noted at Barncluith 'a very romantic garden with terras-villas, banqueting houses, with walls and grottos and all of them filled with large evergreens, in the shapes of beasts and birds', but commented wryly that water works and Dutch topiary work, in 'shapes of beasts and birds' and other forms, were not to everyone's taste. Elements of

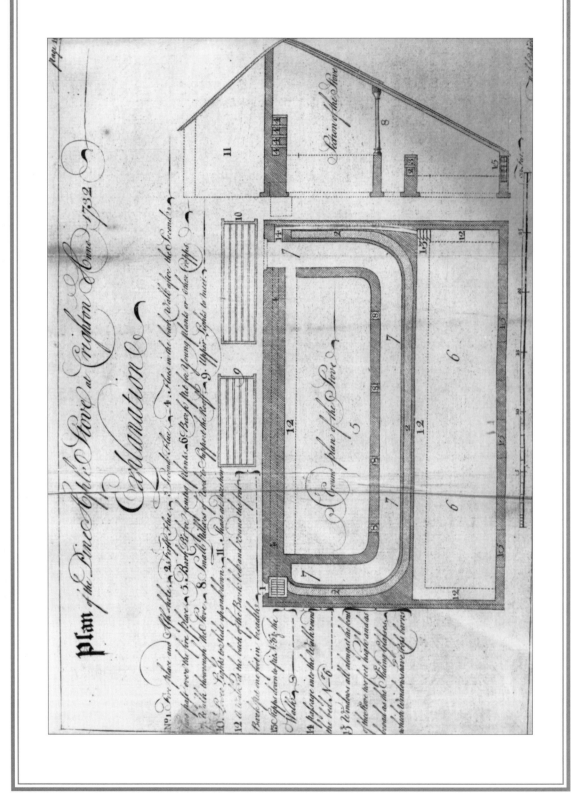

Drumlanrig and Barncluith suggest the Franco-Dutch tradition favoured by William and Mary that bridged the Renaissance and the Baroque: topiary, 'greens' in tubs, canal systems lined with hedges.

Less elevated and affluent members of the nobility and gentry created relatively modest landscapes, some with the help of designers and some with the inspiration of members of the family who had travelled in England and abroad or studied the latest literature: D'Argenville's *Théorie et pratique du jardinage* (1709), perhaps, Addison's *Spectator* essays on the pleasures of the imagination (1712), Pope's *Guardian* essays on topiary (1713), Batty Langley's *New Principles of Gardening* (1728), Philip Miller's *Gardeners Dictionary* (1731).

'But people who made it their business to lay out ground for gentlemen, are, in my opinion, very unfit for it, for they are too formal and stiff' wrote the 6th Earl of Haddington; 'besides, they make everything so busy, that they crowd the ground too much.'

William Adam's plan for Arniston House c.1726 (and earlier, his design for Newliston, built later by his son Robert Adam) is one of several that demonstrate his contribution to garden and estate design. Seaton Delaval Hall in Northumberland (thought to be the work of William Etty), Newliston and Arniston share a similar layout to one of the designs shown by Dezallier d'Argenville in *The Theory and Practice of Gardening*: 'the garden plan is roughly square and surrounded by a raised terrace walk with bastions at the corners. A canal formed from a stream runs east to west though the centre of the square until it curves north of the parterre and house.' At Arniston the parterre terminates in a circular basin and *jet d'eau*. Walks and sight lines from the house form the main axis of the design in all three schemes (Arniston, Seaton Delaval and Newliston) and woodland is an important common component through which subsidiary walks, some serpentine, lead through densely planted areas.

John Reid's *The Scots Gard'ner* had been the first Scottish gardening book. Now others followed: John James's translation into English of D'Argenville's *The Theory and Practice of Gardening* (1712), James Justice's *The Scots Gardiners Director* (1754) and *The British Gardeners Calendar* (1759), inspired by Reid's book and calendar both published in Edinburgh in 1683. In an era gripped by horticultural fervour botanists and gardeners were eager to learn anything and

Opposite.
'All my Exoticks are in a mighty prosperous thriving condition in the Stoves as well as the greenhouse,' wrote James Justice, who included his 1732 plan for the Crichton pineapple stove in his influential handbook, *The Scots Gardiners Director.*

everything about plant, shrub and tree species and what would and would not flourish in the various microclimates and soils of Scotland. Slowly but surely knowledge spread about what could and could not be grown in Scotland, and naturally, mistakes were made. One of the earliest monkey puzzle trees was protected in a conservatory at Blair Castle for its first 20 years before others had demonstrated the tree's ability to withstand the climate of many parts of Scotland very well. The titles of Justice's publications were qualified with 'particularly adapted to the Climate of Scotland' and 'chiefly adapted to the Climate of North Britain'. Justice's *Calendar* was intended to direct 'the Necessary Works in Every Month in the Kitchen, Fruit, and Pleasure Gardens, and in the Nursery, Greenhouse and Stove, to which is added a Dissertation on Forest Trees and a catalogue of Seeds, Roots &c'.

Kitchen gardens were all the rage with the growing band of amateur gardeners whom Justice had in mind as readers of his works. Rather than leave the garden entirely to the gardener, members of the 'middling sort' often liked to put in the spade themselves and dig in the new plants to mingle with old favourites in an artful way. Justice's *The Scots Gardeners Director* contained explicit instructions for 'those Gardiners, who make a Kitchen Garden and the Culture of Flowers their Business'. He was an authority with friends in the highest botanical reaches and had become a Fellow of the Royal Society in 1730. His own garden was full of floricultural wonders and famous in its day, its operation and maintenance meticulously recorded in the diaries and publications so that it is possible to reconstruct his world on various levels, from the 'florists' flowers' he grew to the garden tools he used, as well as methods for cultivating 'Exoticks' in glasshouses or against hot walls. He was so keen on tulips that contemporaries called him a 'tulipmaniac'.

Justice's zeal in obtaining plants is reminiscent of James Sutherland's in the previous generation, but Justice's modus operandi was more scientific and more commercial. He had local suppliers in the Edinburgh nurseries of Archibald Eagle, William Boutcher, Patrick Drummond and William Borthwick; he obtained cauliflower and pineapple plants from James Scot of Turnham Green, London; a correspondent in Italy sent him *finochia* seed every year; he travelled twice to the Continent, saw innovative methods of horticulture at first hand in Haarlem, Brussels and Rotterdam, and visited gardeners at Montreuil and Aix-en-Provence where he learned about peach cultivation. He could converse in Dutch and French, had a knowledge of Latin and wrote 'in a literary, rather pedantic style of English typical of the age'. His contacts included the highest in the land, great landowners such as the Duke of Argyll and the Marquess of Rockingham; he knew Lord Milton, the Fletchers of Saltoun and Sir Hew Dalrymple of North Berwick, lawyers including David Home, and a wide circle of burgesses and merchants.

Like his grandfather, Sir John Foulis, James Justice became an active member of the Honourable Society of Improvers in the Knowledge of Agriculture in Scotland, founded in 1723, which soon attracted almost three hundred members of the Scottish aristocracy, gentry, professionals, merchants and shopkeepers. The members tended to be landowners who stood to profit by land exploitation but they had serious intentions to improve the welfare of the community and put Scotland 'on the map' economically. Treatises laid down many of the new agricultural theories which would be taken up with fervour later in the century. The Duke of Perth (1648–1716) at Drummond Castle had been an early leader in the agricultural reforms; one of the most famous later leaders was John, 4th Duke of Atholl, nicknamed the 'Planting Duke', who developed his estates from 1774 until his death in 1830.

Following Daniel Defoe's trip to Scotland in 1710, Scots had been able to take advantage of the free trading which developed after the Union, and despite further turmoil at the time of Prince Charles Edward Stewart these improvements continued. Even as the Jacobite issue split the country, and the established women of Edinburgh bedecked with breast-knots and favours entertained Prince Charles at their private assemblies, many of their menfolk wagered on the government side, preferring to consider revolutionary ideas for increasing crop yields, and improving land drainage and methods of husbandry, including pasture improvement. In those days, as it was a century later at the time of Robert Louis Stevenson, Edinburgh was part capital and part country town; many of the elite residents of the Old Town and early New Town were owners of country seats.

According to John Loudon, the garden historian and popularist: 'The

best garden in Scotland, about the beginning of the eighteenth century was that of James Justice, at Crichton, near Edinburgh.' Thanks to the painstaking research of garden historian Priscilla Minay, James Justice springs vividly to life on the other side of the red sandstone walls of Crichton House, where the passionate plantsman gardened and carried out experiments to produce 'flour [flower] seeds' and 'firr seeds'. She writes that he was

> boy-like in his enthusiasm for gardening … a visionary believer in the possible greatness of his native land and an exhorter of its people to ever greater things. He was infected by the true spirit of the age in which he lived – that of 'Improvement' – and which he had indeed seen demonstrated as a boy, personified in the figure of his grandfather, Sir James Foulis of Ravelston and Woodhall.

In his capacity as gardening adviser to the 'greit and good' he wrote many letters: 'I should beg you would order your Gardiner to sow all them flour [flower] seeds I sent out in straight lines Drawn across the borders well made up for yt Purpose.' And, in another letter:

> In Planting Season I generally observe one ought to remember one's promises Especially in Flours, for which reason as I promised Please receive from this bearer four small paper bags of Flour roots viz: six roots of fine double white hyacinths, twelve roots of Polyanthos Orientall Narcissus 20 roots fine Anemonies and 40 roots fine Persian Ranunculus The Hyacinths and Orientall narcissus must be planted immediately on a South border 4 inches deep in the Ground. The Anemonies & Ranunculus must be planted in the same border 2½ inches Deep. As you are but a beginner and a young Brother Gardiner I must see your Sucess in these roots which I put in your hands for a tryall of skill and according to your performance you may expect flours of greater beautie and value.

Crichton House garden in James Justice's day sounds like an earthly paradise. One longs to time-travel back to it with its scents and birdsong, earth-clodded spades and trowels and greenhouse smells of seeds and green twine. Sadly, his days in paradise came to an abrupt end and his last years were spent, clouded by poverty, in Leith. The financial value of plants and bulbs was a consideration of the day, as the newspaper advertisement inserted by Drummond and Co. after his death poignantly emphasises:

> The late Mr JUSTICE's valuable and curious COLLECTION of AURICULAS, polyanthus, Tulips, Hyacinths, Ranunculus, Anemonies, Iris's etc, ALSO, just now arrived from Holland, as usual, a large assortment of FLOWER ROOTS, for planting in gardens, and to flower on water glasses.

Better to remember him in his heyday, planting, writing, experimenting, and particularly concerned with propagating hyacinths for which he advocated a compost made up of 'Sea-sand' and 'cows dung'. Compost was a compelling interest. He had seen at first hand in Holland the difference good compost made to blooms and went so far as to import some himself. Perhaps this is not so strange, since fertiliser is known to have been brought back in the holds of ships from the Low Countries as ballast to lands as far north as Morayshire.

In *The Scots Gardiners Director* Justice describes a planting arrangement he favoured for a border: tall spikes of *fritillaries* poking through a bed of *Erythronium denscanis*, the dog's-tooth violet. His design included two or three rows, each interspersed with different sorts of fritillaries selected from the Dutch 'Mynheers *Voorhelms* Catalogues'. Some fritillaries he raised from seed himself, much to his delight. Varieties of crown imperials (*Fritillaria imperialis*), China aster (*Callistephus chinensis*), *Anemone hepatica* and the Persian iris absorbed Justice's skills. But Priscilla Minay says that above all his beloved 'Florist's flours' the auricula took pride of place after the double hyacinth and tulip. He was meticulous in auricula cultivation and knew exactly what he wanted:

> a strong erect Stem, short Pedicles, different Colours (or painted ones) being well and distinctly marked, with round,

Scotland's unique architectural celebration of the fruit: The Pineapple, Stirlingshire (whose designer is unknown), was built in 1761 for the 4th Earl of Dunmore as a folly and garden retreat.

Reprinted by permission of the National Trust for Scotland.

florid, large Eyes, together with well expanded Bells, which must not croud upon one another but must show themselves distinctly, with a handsome narrow Funnel inclosing well proportioned Stamina.

Once he planted auriculas out in long borders for nosegays and eventually he wrote that he was not alone in judging that he 'exceeded all the Blows [flowerings] of any Auriculas ever seen in Scotland, in England, or in Europe'.

Justice and Philip Miller corresponded and exchanged plants. Philip Miller had become immensely important in his field as writer, horticultural botanist, plant collector and adviser to the great, and under his direction the Chelsea Physic Garden became the most richly stocked garden in the world. The two botanists discussed in their letters ways to handle exotic and tender plants in the Scottish climate:

The spring is now advancing if any extraordinar occurs, shall communicate it to you [writes Justice]. I have a pretty promising aspect in my Gardens of some new beauties, I have 8 of the Ananas [pineapples] in fine fruit, many of the Coffee berries of a fine Cherry colour upon the tree … The Guajavas are preparing for blossom: in short all my Exoticks are in a mighty prosperous thriving condition in the Stoves as well as the greenhouse.

The letter, written in 1730, describing pineapples which take one to two years to fruit proves the existence of stoves and greenhouses in Scotland at least as early as 1727–8. James Justice claims to have been the first to fruit pineapples in Scotland using tan bark pits as hot beds for the pines, a method Philip Miller had introduced to the Chelsea Physic Garden. Justice included his own plans for the 1732 Crichton pineapple stove in

his *Director* which, with the introduction of windows at either end, suggests the progenitor of the lean-to greenhouses that would become widely used in the walled gardens of estates.

The cultivation of the fascinating and delicious pineapple, represented on the title page of John Parkinson's florilegium *Paradisi* in 1629, had become a starry challenge to horticulturalists in the eighteenth century. One method was described in *The History of Succulent Plants* (1717) by Richard Bradley, the pioneer of garden journalism, and by the 1730s the challenge had been met by cognoscenti such as Alexander Pope. Scotland's unique architectural celebration of the fruit, The Pineapple, Stirlingshire (whose designer is unknown), was built in 1761 for the 4th Earl of Dunmore as a folly and garden retreat. The astonishing building, of international importance, replicates the fruit with its leaf crown and forms the central pavilion feature of the north garden wall. The walls of the garden are of Scottish design with a double-flued heating wall. Presumably the Dunmores were mad about pineapples and they, too, may have cultivated them in tan bark pits.

James Justice's contemporary, Sir John Clerk (1676–1755), 2nd Baronet of Penicuik, was gripped with the horticultural fervour that swept Britain in the eighteenth century. *Furor hortensis* had many facets: floriculture, horticulture, 'landskip' improvements, art and poetry, and one of its main tap roots can be traced to the tourism that became popular after the Peace of Utrecht (1715) made travel in Europe safer and easier. Privileged young men – Robert Adam, the architect, was one – were accompanied by distinguished tutors or 'bear leaders' such as Thomas Hobbes, Adam Smith and Joseph Addison, who were responsible for the instruction and moral and religious development of their charges whose ultimate destination was Italy. The grand tour across the Alps was fraught with danger and discomfort. *Banditti* threatened the primitive roads and Barbary pirates the high seas, wolves and bears roamed the mountains, inns were squalid. Yet risk was an essential aspect of the adventure, and specialised guides were produced, including Thomas Nugent's *The Grand Tour: Containing an Exact Description of Most of the Cities, Towns, and Remarkable Places of Europe* (1743).

Sir John Clerk travelled in Italy and in 1728 was listed among the subscribers to Robert Castell's *Villas of the Ancients Illustrated*. The book was dedicated to Richard Boyle, 3rd Earl of Burlington, chief patron of the Palladian revival, whose country house at Chiswick had been modelled on Palladio's Villa Rotunda. A member of the Society of Antiquaries in London, Clerk knew Burlington and is likely to have discussed his poetical memoir *A Countryman's Diary*, which he started to write in 1726 as an expression of his feeling for the pastoral and poetical inherent in landscape. Both the poem and the layout of his own estates were influenced by the tours Clerk made, not only on the Continent, but to the most progressive gardens in Scotland and England. He identified four main categories of domestic buildings according to the standing and financial means of the owner – Royal Palace, House of State, Useful House and Villa – which should be built according to 'how the antients formd their rural Seats'. He also advised on the layout of the surrounding grounds, stressing in *A Countryman's Diary*:

> The darling Country Seat must only be
> Where good and Bounteous Nature seems inclin'd
> By moderate Culture to reward our Pains.

The houses of the rural poor were not fit for even the enlightened gentleman's consideration. In 1769 Thomas Pennant wrote that they 'look at a distance like so many black mole-hills'. Pennant found thriving pockets of industry in the Highlands 'owing to the abolition of feudal tenures, or vassalage; for before that was efected … the strong oppressed the Weak, the Rich the Poor'. At Inveraray, in sad contrast to the wealth of its Inveraray Castle, he saw 'the most wretched hovels that can be imagined'. At Lochaber he found people living in structures framed with upright wattle poles, the roofs 'formed of boughs like a wigwam, and the whole is covered with sods; so that in this moist climate their cottages have a perpetual and much finer verdure than the rest of the country'. It would be a long time before descendants of the destitute had gardens of note.

Meanwhile, in England, subtle sects were influencing the landscape movement. Two of the leaders were the architect-designer

William Kent (1685–1748) and the country gentleman Phillip Southcote (1698–1758). It was Kent who, in the words of Horace Walpole, 'leaped the fence, and saw that all nature was a garden'. And Kent made the dictum of his friend Alexander Pope his own: 'all gardening is landscape painting.' Garden design, freed of formality, could now reflect Elysium where the gods themselves might be pleased to dwell. Southcote's desire was rather to create Arcadian landscapes where, as Miles Hadfield puts it: 'mortal Strephons and Uranias, Phillidas and Corydons, slip in and out of … [the ideal countryside]'.

When Clerk of Penicuik visited Corby Castle, Yorkshire, it was owned by Thomas Howard, 'one of the first persons who broke through the trammels of the ancient style of laying out grounds', according to Loudon. Clerk wrote that Howard had shown him 'a passage in the 4th book of Milton's paradise [Lost] where he describes the Garden of Eden which very near resembles the description one wou'd give of Corby Castle'. Enraptured by what he saw at Corby in 1734 Clerk wrote:

> I think no place of my acquaintance in Britain is equal to it ....
> The house stands on a promontary of rock overlooking the
> River Eden … [which is] covered with wood on both sides …
> there are some artificial grotos … on the River side is a large
> walk … beautified all along with grotoes & Statues of the
> Rural deities, at the end of this walk next the house is a
> Cascade 140 feet high.

Elysium, Arcady, Eden, 'Antient Paradise': heady metaphors for the Baron's consideration. He had more than one country seat to plot and in the 1720s had worked on Mavisbank, Loanhead, with William Adam. The house, in the classical style (now in a lamentable state of dereliction), was completed by 1727 and made an unforgettable impression on visitors: 'you would there think yourself rather in a valley near Tivoli than Edenborough,' declared Robert Gale, Clerk's antiquarian friend. At Mavisbank, Gale noted the kitchen garden, 'a great circle, walled in, in the bottome of a steep valley, surrounded with a fine, rapid river, & gives a most beautifull prospect of the house & other gardens above it'. Nearly everything had gone to rack and ruin at

A plan of the landscape at Penicuik House by John Laurie (1757).

Reproduced by permission of National Archives of Scotland, RHP 9375 and Sir John Clerk of Penicuik.

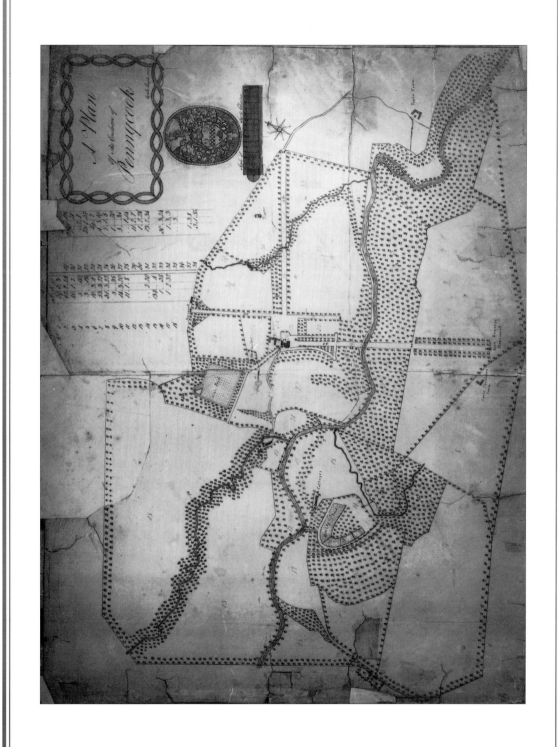

Mavisbank at the beginning of the twenty-first century. Presumably Mavisbank once had a glorious parterre. Clerk's poetical words from *A Countryman's Diary* take on the magical ring of a long-lost past, and stand repeating as a memorial to Mavisbank:

> Around the Fabrick spread the wide Parterre
> Like to a verdant Mantle edgd with Gold
> Or an embroyderd Carpet all perfumd
> With Indian Sweets, here with a mystick mien.

Content with Mavisbank and its garden, but with an eye to the future when he would inherit Newbiggin at nearby Penicuik (his grandfather's towerhouse home since 1646), Clerk had started to garden and design the landscape there, where the gardens were typical of the previous century and included a simple bowling green. Eventually he linked this garden to the landscape by way of a short cut that began a circular walk to the Cave of Hurley and back to the house by a different route.

> This country domain of mine is distinguished by many enclosures and preserves, and is everywhere fed with springs and rivulets [Sir John wrote]. Some 500 acres give employment to my servants. Part is destined for pasturage, part for hay, and part for grain. Here, too, the variety greatly pleases the eye – plantations of timber forest trees, hills and rocks interspersed, covered with shrubs and thickets, nor are there wanting rugged and contorted boulders, those relics of an ancient world which, if not terrible of aspect, adorn the face of nature.

The landscape was perfect for the picturesque treatment and, as for gardens, he had recommendations to make:

> Whether with stony wall, or thorny hedge
> You fence your Garden round, be always sure
> To keep each lovely Object still in Sight:
> But shun the artless Practise to expose
> Your Fields at once to any single View.

Sir John Clerk, outstanding eighteenth-century landowner and dilettante, took up landscape design with such fervour that his activities might be termed 'artistic process'. First of all the process engaged his imagination. He dwelled on his task with philosophical intelligence and poetical rapture, yet his canniness (sound good sense) prevented him from being carried away by *furor hortensis*: 'This a beuty to see things naturel & at Little or no expence,' he declared. 'All expensive ornaments about Gentlemen's houses are so shocking that those who see them commonly bless thimselves that they do not belong to them.'

Indeed, the Baron of Penicuik's state of mind with regard to improvement seems to exhibit the three faculties extolled by treatises of the time: sense, imagination and understanding. Sense was explained as a faculty that allows ideas of things to be summoned up while no longer in their presence (a reminder of the art of memory). David Hume argued that understanding helps form our conception of a world of enduring objects independent of our experience, and Joseph Addison had written the quintessential work on gardening and imagination in a series of eleven essays 'On the Pleasure of the Imagination' for the *Spectator* by 1712. Sight, Addison insisted, 'the most perfect and most delightful of all our Senses' provides imagination with its ideas. In his essays, he cites landscapes as sources of pleasures for the imagination. His observations influenced the ethos of the Grand Tour. Art appreciation and the acquisition of art were the main focus of the tour. Although Italian masters such as Pompeo Batoni still painted many young travellers, portraiture – the most popular genre of seventeenth-century Britain – gave way to a new appetite for landscape painting, particularly by French and Italian masters who reflected the glory of the Alps and the Roman campagna in their canvases. Salvator Rosa's rugged, romantic scenes reminded them of their own arduous travels. Nicolas Poussin and Claude Lorrain perfectly expressed the Arcadian landscapes of Italy's classical heritage, and, later in the century, Gaspard Dughet's affinity with the picturesque introduced yet another painterly view of landscape.

Touring caught on in Britain, too, where one guide book promised to reveal astonishing sights to the traveller: 'from the delicate touches of *Claude*, verified on *Coniston* Lake, to the noble scenes of *Poussin*, exhibited in *Windermer*-water, and from there to the

On the next three pages.
Scots Arcadia: the
classical ruin of Penicuik
House; Arthur's O'on in
the converted stable block;
Lions guardants.

stupendous romantic ideas of *Salvator Rosa*, realized in the Lake of *Derwent'*.

In Scotland there was a vogue for 'landskips' in interior decoration. The firm of James Norie (1684–1757), and later his son of the same name, most famously produced over-door and overmantle landscape paintings for neo-classical houses, including Newhailes, Midlothian, and houses in the Canongate of Edinburgh, including one at Chessels Court. Typically, the paintings showed the ruins of a classical building set in a landscape, perhaps with a city in the distance, following the Continental practice. The work is provincial, unsophisticated and intended as decoration rather than great art. The dominant, muted grey and green paints selected ensured that, rather than standing out assertively, the work took its place in the overall decoration of a room.

The Lake District, the Wye Valley, the Welsh mountains and the Scottish Highlands were favourite British tourist destinations, where visitors were encouraged not only to imagine the landscape through the eyes of the painters they admired, but also to attempt their own representations of the landscape. Guide books identified 'station points' near picturesque views. Drawing tools and watercolour sets as well as a Claude glass for framing the view were standard equipment of British tourists (the term 'tourist' came into use in the late eighteenth century). Nowadays, the camera is the substitute Claude glass; there is no need to make our own depictions of the landscape. This is both a convenience and a loss, for nowadays we seldom look properly at anything, let alone absorb a view into our very being by the act of drawing it or painting it.

Today the grounds of Penicuik House, described by their creator as 'pleasant rather than sumptuous', look ravishing in autumn dress. The house is another matter, a gaunt ruin (destroyed by fire in 1899). Newbiggin, transformed into Old Penicuik House by Sir John's son, James (1761–9), shortly after the old man's death, was considered one of the marvels of the day and, in our time, it has been called 'the ideal of a Scottish Palladian House'. Nowadays it is the grounds visitors come to see and stroll around, unless they exert their most vivid imaginations to recreate the poignant ruin as a villa in the Roman style. Clerk's descendant, Sir John, lives in New Penicuik House with his

wife, Lady Clerk. Their courtyard mansion was converted from the 1760 stables and estate offices after the fire. A domed doocot, Arthur's O'on [Oven], dominates the courtyard (a reproduction of one which stood on the banks of the River Carron in Stirlingshire until 1743). The Clerks have received me kindly with coffee and homemade shortbread, we have studied maps of the estate, then I am on my way, hoping that they find in their retreat as the Baron did: 'the most profound and undisturbed ease' and I wonder if they hear old echoes of their illustrious ancestor's poetry blowing in the wind:

> Let Nature in the Pride of blooming Flowrs
> Triumphant sit, and all the Gardiners Toils
> Direct with matchless grace.

A Countryman's Diary is certainly in my mind as I follow Sir John's directions along a straight path through the woods to the High Pond with its fine views of the Pentland Hills, its waters thronged with dabbling ducks:

> Let many lofty Trees with Spreading Tops
> Defend you from the Cold of Northern Blasts
> Let here and there be seen some little Hills
> Fit Pasture for your harmless bleating Flocks.

Retracing my steps, the Alan Ramsay Monument (erected after his father's death by Clerk's son, James) is in the frame of the camera lens as I walk up the avenue:

> The Avenue will most delight the Sight
> That on some beauteous object shapes its way
> Such is a temple whose high towring Spire
> Divides the ho'vring Clouds and seems to be
> A lofty Pillar to support the Heavns.

I think as I stroll, two things: that some of the avenue's obscuring trees require pruning, the better to honour John Clerk's intentions; and that the book and the journey are drawing to a close. Still, it is better to

stroll to the end of a journey when the future beckons, even if such tantalising delights as the nearby garden at Newhall, Carlops, must wait for another venture. Sir John Clerk was associated with Newhall in his later years, as was his friend, the poet Allan Ramsay, who set his celebrated dramatic poem, 'The Gentle Shepherd', there. In the Glen of the North Esk lie its ruined memorials: 'Habbie's How', 'Peggy's Poo' and 'Craigie Beild'. Anyone who wants to see a fine eighteenth-century Scottish walled garden, complete with shrubs, kitchen garden, lily pool melon pit, peach house and vinery, should visit Newhall.

Sir John Clerk took delight in all the arts. Influential London wits like Lord Burlington were included in his circle, the Academia dell'Arcadia, which attracted cultured Scots including William Adam, Allan Ramsay and his painter son. The poetical centrepiece at the heart of 'Clerkland', his landscape at Penicuik, is the cave, or grotto, and the pond of Hurley which I hope to find now. Clerk thought the walk along the Esk, which he spanned with the Centurion's Bridge, echoed Corby's 'Eden' and he intended to construct cascades a hundred feet high on both banks. Beyond me lies Hurley Park with a narrow steep-sided circular valley lying at a rise called Claremont where Clerk planned to build a Gothic tower. Here, on the riverbank he cut the mouth of his 'frightful cave or Grotto', which I search for now among squelching moss and fern.

'I use as much exercise as my Bodily strength will allow of, for I generally walk a Mile or two every day,' he noted in his seventy-fifth year. 'My constant walk is my pond of Hurley and [its] Grotto, where I take great delight.'

Sir John's approach to the grotto was easier than mine. There are the ruined caissons that once held a stout bridge across the Esk, surely Clerk's idea of the River Styx. Across the bridge, steps led him to the entrance, as if to the entrance of the underworld (now regarded as dangerous and shut with a padlocked gate). The entrance is, as he wrote:

> Noteworthy for its position and solitude, which a poet only
> could describe. It is surrounded by hills and steep rocks, and
> no one can get access to it but by the mouth of a frightful cave.
> To those who enter, therefore, first occurs the memory of the

cave of the Cuman Sibyl, for the ruinous aperture, blocked up
with stones and briars, strikes the eye. Then there comes upon
the wayfarer a shudder, as they stand in doubt whether they
are coming among the living or the dead.

I cannot follow in through the aperture, up the sloping passage he
constructed that leads underground into a chamber that bears the
punning admonition *Tenebrosa Occultaque Cave* – 'Beware of dark and
hidden things' – yet easily I conjure up the old man, touching in his
enthusiasm for his daily rehearsal of death. Yes, there he is, going in
under the arch with the help of his stick. It would be a shepherd's
crook, I imagine. What I can do is climb up over the hill, over twisting
roots and ferny foliage reminiscent of Tennell's illustrations for *Alice in
Wonderland*, above Sir John's underground passage, slipping and
slithering to the other side, taking his word for it, that in the
underground passage below:

> certain discords set off give finish to musical cadences in such
> a way as to render the subsequent harmony grateful to the ear,
> so does the form of this mournful cave, with its long and
> shady path followed by the light and prospect, make the exit
> more delightful.

Sure enough, I have arrived at the exit from the underworld (also shut
up with a gate) with its glimpse of paradise, the calm, sheltered lochan
called Hurley Pond. I see the old man coming out, transformed and
renewed by his adventure, rewarded by this glimpse of paradise: 'For
sudden the darkness disappears, and as it were at the creation of a new
world.'

CHAPTER 10

'Improvement'

THE HEDGES WERE CUT DOWN, THE TREES STUBBED UP,

AND THE WHOLE CHARACTER OF THE PLACE SO MUCH DESTROYED

THAT WE WERE GLAD WHEN WE COULD LEAVE IT

As international trade increased, the reformers of the first agricultural society were often to the fore in trading with the colonies, especially in the Far East, Africa and America, and some of its members played an important part in bringing back to Scotland hundreds of new plants and trees. Interest in the potential economic value of exotic plants gave birth to the Society for the Importation of Foreign Seed (1765), which specialised in seeds from North America. New species were introduced and treasured by their cultivators. James Justice described his scientific approach to 'Cape of Good Hope' plants in the 1759 *Calendar*, whose 'fibres played at great pleasure among the different sorts of earth' in a heated greenhouse. Between the first and eighth editions of Philip Miller's *Gardeners Dictionary* the number of plants cultivated in England had multiplied five times. Miller was an avid collector and received 'booty' from America, the West Indies and the Cape of Good Hope as well as Europe and Scotland. In the eighth edition of the *Dictionary* (1768) he adopted the binomial system, by which plants had a one-word generic name and a single specific epithet, as recommended by Carl Linnaeus in 1753.

A century's evolution of the art of gardening had trained hundreds of Scots gardeners working under the eye of land masters, architects and gentry. Estate gardeners were excellently placed to supply seed and plants to neighbouring cottagers and their friends who would be just as keen as higher-born folk to cultivate their own vegetable and flower plots. Plants like polyanthus, wallflower, London pride, thyme, spearmint and southernwood, suited to the soil and climate, flourished. But the humble marigold was the most popular plant. Either that or marigolds spread faster than other garden plants, and in some areas became such a 'menace' that cottagers who let them get out of control could be fined, according to a clause inserted in their leases.

There was no shortage of trained gardeners – a love of gardening seems to run like a love of landscape, song and poetry in the Scottish blood – even though at the beginning of the eighteenth century many had emigrated across the Border. Indeed, one of the most fruitful clues to the existence of substantial numbers of elaborate early gardens in Scotland *well before* the Union is the existence of those gardeners referred to in British garden histories. The evidence exists and stands repeating. Early Scottish gardens kept pace with the rest of Europe, only many of those gardens went missing. Unlike paintings, antiques and other interior furnishings, gardens are ephemeral, organic life forms that erupt then decay from season to season and year to year and depend on consistent management.

We must refute the assertion that Scotland had no gardens to speak of before Union. 'As early as the 1700s a sizable emigration of Scots gardeners crossed the Border to seek work on English estates,' we read. But where had they come from if there were no gardens to speak of in Scotland? These gardeners did not happen to appear overnight, fully trained, cap in hand. Their own gardens had disappeared after the Reformation, or had become neglected by the drain of their owners to London or to other Scottish estates. Thomas, 6th Earl of Haddington, returned to Tyninghame around 1700 after the estate had been let out for many years to find the garden ruined: 'hedges uptrooted, mounds and banks ploughed level'.

The Earl and his wife were great landscapers and subsequently employed many gardeners but others were not so fortunate. Hundreds of trained gardeners had to find work in the south and more than one aristocrat cried out that he would have no other head gardener but a Scot on his English estate. At the time many of the top curators, botanists and horticulturalists in England and on the Continent were Scots or of Scots descent, who helped their country's gardeners to find work. They were experts, these gardening men, and had learned their skills at the knee of parents and grandparents who had worked, as we have seen, at the side of head gardeners (some French or Italian) on Scottish estates for well over a century. They knew the value of good soil and how to prepare it, how to nurse the tenderest plants and how to propagate the toughest.

Later, so many Scots jumped over the walls of their English gardens into the nursery trade in London that their presence became an issue: 'The English in retaliation rushed into print and attacked Scottish gardeners tooth and nail,' asserts E. H. M. Cox in *A History of Gardening in Scotland* (1935). But as the century progressed, horticulture in all its forms expanded and the storm in a teacup abated. There was plenty of work on both sides of the Border for everyone who

wanted to succeed. 'It is true both in agriculture and horticulture that a man will naturally tend to drift to a softer and more equable climate, where conditions are easier and plants of all kinds respond more rapidly to care and attention,' Cox reflected. There was, of course, much more to it than that. The southwards drift of so many Scots gardeners was encouraged by the energetic network of well-placed Scottish horticulturalists in England and on the Continent as well as by the monumental reforms of wealthy landowners who kept estates on both sides of the Border.

It was a northerner, Lancelot 'Capability' Brown (1715–83), who changed the face of England with his 'visionary' designed landscapes. Brown influenced several gardens in his native Northumberland in the course of his career, but, although his influence was felt in Scotland, he never crossed the Border to work on Scottish landscapes. 'Capability' Brown's schemes were exceedingly labour-intensive. Teams of gardeners widened English rivers, created lakes, moved earth to alter the contours of parklands and planted groves, hanging woods and encircling belts of perimeter trees. Entire valleys were affected by ambitious schemes, settlements were resited and tens of thousands of trees were planted. The Duke of Argyll even had a village removed to improve the view at one of his English estates. Many of the gardeners who laboured on such Promethean schemes were drawn from the hundreds of Scots who crossed the Border from the beginning of the century while, back home, Scotland held back on the excesses of improvement.

Consciousness of the new English landscape style was tempered by the majestic natural landscape of much of Scotland. Owners of houses in the Scottish countryside had natural features to grapple with that were unknown in gentler parts of England: mountains for a start, or hills, great rushing rivers, waterfalls, boulders, scree, ravines, gulleys – natural features that were more than a match for most landscape contrivances. In Scotland, wildernesses didn't have to be created. Wildernesses *were*. So, while trendsetting landowners north of the Border such as John Clerk of Penicuik adopted some of the precepts of landscape style, his was a poetic interpretation, full of allusion as paradises are.

The head gardener at Blenheim was a Scot in Alexander Carlyle of Inveresk's day (1722–1805). In his autobiography Carlyle notes: 'at Bulstrode we discovered the truth of what I had often heard, that most of the head-gardeners of English noblemen were Scotch.' Did they, as Cox suggests, consider that 'a man who has been trained in an unkindly climate will by nature work harder than one who has lived all his life under comparatively easier conditions'? Gardening, he notes, attracts

> an excellent type of man, not afraid to work with his own hands, however high his position, a good organizer, self-reliant and thoroughly trustworthy. If some may have been a trifle lacking in imagination and have been dour, yet they were often saved by a pawky humour.

The emigration of Scots gardeners increased under the influence of Philip Miller, who made no bones about preferring to work with his own countrymen. Many served apprenticeships in England and went on to fill the good positions he obtained for them. Lord Petre's famous gardener, John Gordon, was described to Carl Linnaeus as having 'more knowledge in vegetation than all the gardeners and writers on gardening in England put together, but he is too modest to publish anything. If you send him anything rare, he will make you a proper return'. Peter Collinson remarked that Gordon had 'a sagacity peculiar to himself' and judged James Lee of Selkirk 'not far behind him'. When he was about seventeen years old in 1732, Lee walked south over the Border, 'carrying his sword' until his journey was broken to recover from smallpox at Litchfield. He was employed at Syon and later by the Duke of Argyll at Whitton before he became a partner in a London nursery. Lee published his *Introduction to Botany* (1760) with an explanation of the new Linnaean binomial system: the 'sexual' classification of plants based on the number of stamens and stigmas found in a flower that is still accepted as the basis for botanical nomenclature. He employed collectors and agents overseas, and valued an important connection with France, partly through Thomas Blaikie, a fellow Scot, who visited Lee in England and brought new plants and orders to the nursery.

Blaikie was born near Corstorphine Hill in 1750 and eventually found his way to France, where he remodelled the Duke of Orleans'

gardens at Monceaux. It had been a passion for plant collecting that first took the young man to France. Later, in his *Diary of a Scotch Gardener* (1775–92), Blaikie claims to have sent back 'most of the plants mentioned in the *Hortus Kewensis* as introduced by others', and though his claim is surely exaggerated he is likely to have sent interesting plants to the Edinburgh botanical garden. Certainly Blaikie was diligent when it came to plant collecting in France and Switzerland, as his diary entries reveal: 'Found exceeding tall the *Sperea Aruncus* and in some of the sides of the Mountains great quantities of the *Rhododendron feruginum*; here I gained towards the Jura … found my old cowherds, went and lodged with them.'

Blaikie also mingled easily in the exalted company of noble employers. Both Voltaire and Marie Antoinette visited the plant collection at his nursery in Paris.

The nursery trade in London became closely associated with the Society of Gardeners (1725), which met monthly to discuss plants, including the new introductions, and to plan plant-hunting trips. Several Scots botanists would become the first plant-hunters later in the century. Philip Miller was clerk to the Society, a position that influenced the publication of his *Gardeners Dictionary*. No doubt the Society of Improvers in the Knowledge of Agriculture in Scotland similarly boosted the trade in the north where nurseries had been established in the previous century, perhaps in emulation of physic gardens.

James Justice, as previously noted, purchased supplies from the Edinburgh nurseries of Eagle, Boutcher, Drummond and Borthwick. Every city supported nurseries such as Urquhart of Dundee, and in Glasgow Robert Austin, partner in McAslan and Austin, founded in 1717 on rented ground at the foot of Hutcheson Street, was supplying plants to Kew Gardens by the end of the century. Austin wrote to Kew's curator William Aiton: 'I have forwarded … per one of the Leith Smacks a parcel containing two plants of each of the varieties of Scots Roses which I have had the good fortune to propagate from seeds.'

Like other nurseries, Robert Austin's firm commissioned paintings to advertise the rarities they held in stock to potential buyers. The *Botanical Magazine*, founded in 1787, abetted the burgeoning nursery trade by illustrating flowers grown by British nurserymen. Nurserymen and seedsmen also advertised their specialities in newspapers. An Edinburgh journal, for example, enticed readers to visit a West Port nursery where 'all sorts of garden seeds … and flowers of the best kinds' were sold in 1721. Old accounts books frequently record the purchase of fruit trees and grafts from nurseries. Sir John Foulis bought fruit trees for under five pounds sterling 'from Ye Gardener in Ye Surgeon's Yard'. His shopping list included: 'a black pippin, a pear dangerous, 2 honie pears, a bon criteon, a swaneg, a bona magna plum'. Newspaper advertisements displayed the variety of goods sold by seedsmen like Drummond from their premises 'at the sign of the Gilded Gardener, opposite to the cross, first stair below the Royal Exchange' in Edinburgh. Here is an edited selection from a Drummond and Co. advertisement:

> Onion, Leek, and great varieties of the best new and fresh grass-seeds … Great Red Topt, Green Topt, and large White-field Turnips, of the best quality. French turnip, Dutch Lintseed, Canary, Rape, Hemp and Maw seeds for birds. All Kinds of Gardeners utensils, Spades polished, and Spanish Steel'd hedge Scissors, and Gloves, Dunse hooks, Reels, etc. Hot-bed mats, Sieves, Bell-glasses, Bird and Flower glasses, Jars for painting, and several sorts of glass-ware, China flower pots, figured Delpht, Dutch ditto, stone ditto, Earthen ditto … Watering Pans, Farnham Hops, Luuca Eating Oil, best Flour of Mustard, whole and Spllit green and white Soft boiling pot-pease, Peppermint-water, Bird-lime, Starch etc.

It is an evocative litany, mainly on the kitchen garden side.

Seedsmen and nurserymen also collected and propagated the huge range of plants that acclimatised well in the north – from sweet williams to asters – but more than anything else, new ways of looking at the landscape stimulated a breathtaking demand for trees. Trees boosted the nursery trade. Although trees had been planted to shelter estate policies at least since 1600 travellers still commented on the lack of woods in the Lowlands. Perhaps they desired or expected to see everywhere in Scotland landscapes resembling the wild places they

marvelled at on the grand tour to Italy? Samuel Johnson suggested planting trees 'to give nature a more cheerful face' after his visit to the Hebrides in 1773. 'To drop seeds into the ground requires little labour and no skill,' he remarked.

Yet the planting of woods and shelterbelts had been a main feature of Scottish estate management for almost two centuries. Landscapers such as Sir William Bruce had instigated avenues of trees at Hopetoun and Bruce's contemporaries, the 6th Earl of Haddington, Thomas Hamilton, and his wife, had been magnificent tree planters who embarked on a forward-looking scheme to protect their policies from the ravaging salt winds of the North Sea near Dunbar. At Tyninghame almost 2 miles of woodland strips and holly hedges traversed avenues of 'millions' of trees, including thirteen riding avenues converging at three arboreal roundabouts, so that Daniel Defoe had been able to marvel at groves grown 'distinguished' by 1727. Thomas Hamilton, in his own words, had been 'a diligent planter for upwards of thirty years, and having more thriving trees of my own raising than I believe any one man planted in his lifetime'. Towards the end of the century the Dukes of Argyll and Atholl would outdo his record, but Haddington's *Some Directions About Raising Forest Trees*, written late in his life, is a lasting testimony to his, and his wife's, contribution.

Tree seeds and saplings had been 'dropped' in great numbers in other parts of Scotland, too, so that by the end of the century travellers appreciated hillsides colonised by trees, enclosed fields, drained low-lying ground now cultivated, country houses and their policies improved with woods and shelterbelts. The agricultural age had arrived in Scotland; and its gardens, orchards and woods flourished, and with them the nursery trade, an established growth industry all over Scotland.

One of the first trade catalogues was printed in 1754 by Patrick Drummond in the Edinburgh Lawnmarket and bound into some copies of James Justice's influential handbook *The Scots Gardiners Director*. The firm of Dicksons in Teviotdale supplied trees to estates in Haddington and Midlothian from 1753. Their wholesale business consisted mostly of whin seed, a shrub as uncommon then as it is ubiquitous now. Larch, Scots pine, laburnum and lime trees for park

and shelterbelt planting were on their lists, as well as more ornamental trees to be planted nearer the house: holly, walnut, elm and crab apple. On smaller estates, where costs prohibited general gardening on any scale, the cultivation and propagation of useful fruit trees increased.

The most prodigious planter of all, though, would be the 4th Duke of Atholl, nicknamed the 'Planting Duke'. Over fourteen million larches and over thirteen million other tree species were planted on his estates between 1774 and 1826. Mr Urquhart, the Dundee nurseryman, had the good fortune to receive an order for fifty thousand one-year-old larches and one million seedling larch in 1824 from the 'Planting Duke', who not only improved his own estate but clothed the surrounding hills of Perthshire with thousands of trees as well, thus creating a picturesque landscape, with his castle at Blair Atholl at the heart of it and Ossian's Folly high above the River Braan a few miles down the road.

Trees and wildness and wet are outstanding features of the landscape the River Braan runs through: a peat-brown silken river tumbling through ravines and gorges, swirling round boulders and fallen trees, occasionally swelling in deep dark pools on its journey from Loch Freuchie in Glen Quaich, the essence of the eighteenth-century untamed Scottish picturesque style.

The 'Planting Duke' of Atholl not only improved his own estate but also clothed the surrounding hills of Perthshire with thousands of trees, thus creating a picturesque landscape with Blair Castle at the heart of it.

Blair Castle (S222) by Colin Baxter © Colin Baxter, reproduced by permission of Colin Baxter Photography Ltd.

Ossian's Hall where
mirrors once covered the
walls and ceilings,
reflecting back the pouring
waterfalls of the River
Braan. The Hermitage
was on the eighteenth-
century tourist map.

© Sheila Mackay, 2001.

Near its destination, its junction with the River Tay, the river displays itself in a spectacular series of rapids and gushing waterfalls, best viewed from the high folly in the Hermitage, constructed in 1758 by the man who would become the 3rd Duke of Atholl. With better roads, visitors arrived in Scotland in greater numbers than ever before, anxious to see the sights. The Hermitage folly was on the tourist map, complete with a ticket system for entry to the elaborately furnished and decorated hall where red and green glass in the windows gave 'a new and surprising effect; turning the water into a cataract of fir, a cascade of liquid verdigrease', as one of these visitors remarked. Towards the end of the eighteenth century the folly was redesigned to be even more amazing, its new name, Ossian's Hall, perfectly echoing rugged romanticism in its modernised interior, where huge mirrors covering the walls and ceilings reflected back the pouring waterfalls of the River Braan. The revival of the Celtic hero Ossian by James Macpherson gripped the imaginations of Scots who, no longer content to be North British, were on the hunt for a distinguishing identity. Elaborate memorials to Ossian appeared in the interior design of grand houses; Penicuik House had painted ceilings by Alexander Runciman in its Ossian's Hall before it was destroyed by fire. Here, beside the waters of the Braan (its very name has an Ossianic ring), one can well imagine the battered warriors of Culchulain in defence of their territory.

A little upriver I find a hermit's cave that was part of the eighteenth-century tourist trail, as it still is today, though empty now. In the mid-seventeenth century it was presented to visitors complete with a real, live Heilanman, suitably attired to play the hermit. And I think of Clerk of Penicuik looking out from his Grotto towards the end of an afternoon, finding 'the natural beauty of the place, and the solitude … a great help to studies and meditation'. As I walk along the riverbank towards my journey's end I think that the classical period after the 1707 Union with England never truly quelled the Scots' love of fantastical wildness. As I scuff through the thick leafmould undercarpet towards Ossian's Hall, I hold that thought, like one of Ariadne's threads, and consider shades of things to come.

In the new world of the second half of the century some artificiality was desirable. Nature had to be tamed, said one of the century's most influential gardeners. Henry Home, Lord Kames (1696–1782), in

Elements of Criticism (1762), attempted to establish principles for the newly fashionable informal style and practised some of them in his gardens at Blair Drummond from 1760. Whatever hour he reached home, he is said to have gone out immediately to look over his garden and plantations, even if it meant carrying a lantern. At Blair Drummond Kames adopted what Sir William Bruce had advocated a century earlier: a degree of formality in the gardens near the house, surrounding woods and parkland. His 'most perfect idea' was to have the various parts arranged 'in such a manner, as to inspire all the different emotions that can be raised by gardening'. He relished, too, the device of the ha-ha, the sunken boundary separating the garden from the parkland leading on to the wilderness. Sir John Clerk's son, James, is credited with constructing one of the first ha-has in Scotland at Old Penicuik House to overlook his father's landscape. It is still there today. From the house, you could view the wilder countryside from windows overlooking parkland grazed by sheep and cows, happy in the knowledge that the ha-ha prevented the animals from coming anywhere near treasured flower and shrub plantings round the house. According to some, the ha-ha had been the *eureka!* that inspired the landscape style of 'Capability' Brown and his contemporaries, permitting as it did uninterrupted vistas by visually connecting foreground, middle distance and background. Brown's ideal of planting for the future might have seemed revolutionary to the English, but Scots already knew the importance of that. 'Capability' Brown's landscape schemes required the planting of thousands of trees but Scottish landowners living in a harsh climate had understood the need for shelterbelts for more than two centuries.

Cox writes that landscape style crept into Scotland in 'its most advanced and poorest forms'. If only people had been sensible and followed the precepts of Lord Kames, he laments, our gardens would be better: 'for the usual "improver" was nothing but a poor imitator and plagiarist of "Capability" Brown in his most destructive mood. They ruined Glamis and a few more gardens north of the Forth, but did more damage in Midlothian and the Border country.'

At Yester by the 1760s the magnificent formal garden had been swept away to be replaced by a 'picturesque design' for which John Adam proposed 'Chinese Bridges and Temples' on the lawns; one or

two trees that might date from the early eighteenth century are the only sad remnants of the great park that so impressed Macky in 1714. On a smaller scale at Blairadam John Adam, too, 'informalised' the parkland his father created and established woodlands including picturesque walks. William Adam's grandson, also William, added clumps and individual parkland trees between 1792 and 1839. Inveraray Castle, Blair Atholl and most of the grandest estates were 'improved'.

Chinoiserie was 'in', an echo of *sharawadgi* in the previous century, this time sounded by the Scot, Sir William Chambers (1726–96), who visited China before setting up as an architect and publishing *Designs of Chinese Buildings* in 1757. Later Chambers raised his head above the classicism he was steeped in to design the pagoda at Kew and to produce *A Dissertation on Oriental Gardening* (1772):

> Their gardeners [the Chinese] are not only botanists, but also painters and philosophers, having a thorough knowledge of the human mind, and the arts by which its strongest feelings are excited …. They observe, that mistakes committed in this art, are too important to be tolerated, being much exposed to view, and in a great measure irreparable; as it often requires the space of a century, to redress the blunders of an hour.

In the second half of the century there were many styles to choose from and precepts to follow as old ways lingered and refused to budge or were superseded and horticultural specimens increased dramatically with the finds brought back from plant-hunters, many of them Scots, sponsored to explore all parts of the globe by the botanical gardens and the largest nurseries.

Lord Kames railed against 'everything unnatural [which] ought to be rejected with disdain … [like] statues of wild beasts vomiting water'. Later, Sir Walter Scott (1771–1832) would agree, preferring a 'production of art' to a 'distortion of nature': 'a stone hewn into a gracefully ornamented vase or urn has a value which it did not before possess; a yew hedge clipped into a fortification is only defaced.' He loved the combination of a traditional walled garden, nearby orchards, a lawn shaded by fine trees, surrounding parks and shelterbelt, all enclosed within a stone boundary wall. He scorned formal gardens which, he said, 'have no more resemblance to that of nature … than the rouge of an antiquated coquette … bears to the artless blush of a cottage girl'. Scott's sort of garden was 'simplicity' itself, not 'affectation labouring to be simple'. He described a favourite garden, planted in around eight acres and

> full of long straight walks … [with] thickets of flowering shrubs, a bower, and an arbour to which access was obtained through a little maze of contorted walks, calling itself a labyrinth … fine ornamental trees … the orchard was filled with fruit-trees of the best description. There were seats and trellis-walks.

Revisiting the garden he had enjoyed at an earlier time in his life, he regretted its so-called 'improvement'. 'Its air of retreat, the seclusion which its alleys afforded, was entirely gone … the hedges were cut down, the trees stubbed up, and the whole character of the place so much destroyed that we were glad when we could leave it.'

Standing above the churning waters of the River Braan on the parapet of Ossian's Folly I have reached the end of my journey and the end of the book. Towards the beginning of the next, there will be Sir Walter Scott and his contemporaries, on the one hand no longer happy to accept the tag 'North British' and, on the other, filled with remorse for the nationhood they once enjoyed and lost after Union, with all its manifestations, including gardens.

APPENDIX I

NOTES ON THE
ART OF MEMORY

The following extracts from Frances A. Yates, *The Art of Memory*, are included here to support the theory that the Edzell Pleasaunce may have links with the sixteenth- and seventeenth-century Theatre Memory systems of Camillo, Bruno, Fludd, Dicson the Scot and others.

Giulio Camillo 'or Giulio Camillo Delmino to give him his full name, was one of the most famous men of the sixteenth-century,' writes Frances Yates.

> He was one of those people whom their contemporaries regard with awe as having vast potentialities. His Theatre was talked of in all Italy and in France; its mysterious fame seemed to grow with the years. Yet what was it exactly? A wooden Theatre, crowded with [memory] images, was shown by Camillo himself in Venice to a correspondent of Erasmus [tutor to the children of the Scottish King James IV and friend of the Scottish scholar, Hector Boece]; something similar was later on view in Paris. The secret of how it really worked was to be revealed to only one person in the world, the King of France. (p. 135)

Giordano Bruno followed the memory system of Camillo in its Renaissance or occult form, of which he knew the secret. **Robert Fludd**, a practitioner of the art of memory, dedicated his *Ultriusque Cosmi ... Historia* to James I and VI during a period when the Renaissance modes of Hermetic and magical thinking were under attack from the rising generation of seventeenth-century philosophers. **Peter Ramus** was a prominent sixteenth-century educational reformer. **Alexander Dicson** 'the Scot' was a member of the Hay family and present in London at the court of James I and VI.

Yates asks:

> Why, when the invention of printing seemed to have made the great Gothic artifical memories of the Middle Ages no longer necessary, was there this recrudescence of the interest in the art of memory in the strange forms in which we find it in the Renaissance systems of Camillo (c.1480–1548) Bruno and Fludd? (p. 12)

Camillo's memory system based on the Seven Pillars of Wisdom transports well to Edzell. So does Bruno's occult memory system presented in his *Spaccio* published in England in 1585, through which the soul was held to have the power magically to animate statues or pictures, specifically of 'the heavens'. Mars, Jupiter, Saturn, Mercury, Venus, Sol and Luna are writ large at Edzell.

The Memory Theatre of Guilio Camillo

When, towards the end of his life, Camillo was at Milan he dictated on seven mornings an outline of his Theatre.

> The Theatre rises in seven grades or steps, which are divided by seven gangways representing the seven planets. The student of it is to be as it were a spectator before whom are placed the seven measures of the world *in spettacolo*, or in a theatre. (p. 141)

> On each of its gangways are seven gates or doors. These gates are decorated with many images … the solitary 'spectator' of the Theatre stands where the stage would be and looks towards the auditorium, gazing at the images on the seven times seven gates on the seven rising grades … the whole system of the Theatre rests basically upon seven pillars, the seven pillars of Solomon's House of Wisdom. (pp. 141–2)

> Solomon in the ninth chapter of *Proverbs* says that wisdom has built herself a house and has founded it on seven pillars. By these columns, signifying most stable eternity, we are to understand the seven Sephiroth of the supercelestial world,

which are the seven measures of the fabric of the celestial and inferior worlds, in which are contained the Ideas of all things both in the celestial and in the inferior worlds. (p. 142)

The plan of Bruno's *Spaccio della bestia trionfante*, published in England in 1585 and dedicated to Sidney [Philip], is based on the images of the forty-eight contellations of the sky, the northern constellations, the zodiac, and the southern constellations. (p. 304)

The 'Expulsion of the Triumphant Beast' [the *Spaccio*] is the expulsion of vice by virtue. (p. 304) [A reference to Protestantism's overthrowal of Roman Catholicism in Northern Europe?]

Nevertheless, the *Spaccio* is very far from being the sermon of a medieval friar on the virtues and vices, rewards and punishments. The personified powers of the soul who conduct the reform of the heavens are JUPITER, JUNO, SATURN, MARS, MERCURY, MINERVA, APOLLO, with his magicians Circe and Medea and his physician Aesculapius, DIANA, VENUS and CUPID, CERES, NEPTUNE, THETIS, MOMUS, ISIS. These figures perceived inwardly in the soul are said to have the appearance of statues or pictures. We are in the realms of the occult memory systems based on magically animated 'statues' as memory images. (p. 306)

In 1584 an extraordinary controvery broke out in England about the art of memory. It was waged between an ardent disciple of Bruno and a Cambridge Ramist. This debate may be one of the most basic of all Elizabethan controversies. And it is only now, at the point in the history of the art of memory which we have reached in this book [*The Art of Memory*] that one can begin to understand what were the issues at stake, what is the meaning of the challenge which Alexander Dicson threw at Ramism from the shadows of ths Brunian art of memory, and why William Perkins angrily retaliated with a defence of the Ramist method as the only true art of memory. (p. 260)

LIST OF PLANTS
GROWING AT ST MARY'S
PLEASANCE, HADDINGTON

Filipendula ulmaria

Onopordum acanthium

Doronicum plantagineum

Borago officinalis

Polemonium caeruleum

Cistus salvifolius

Eupatorium purpureum

Aconitum napellus

Phlomis fruticosa

Acanthus spinosus

Tiarella cordifolia

Epimedium pinnatum

Saxifraga umbrosa

Dianthus alpinus

Rosa alba 'Maxima'

Rosa alba 'Semi-Plena'

Rosa 'Burgundy Rose'

Rosa celsiana

Rosa centifolia

Rosa mundi

Rosa 'Maiden's Blush'

Rosa officinalis

Rosa 'Old Pink Moss'

Artemisia abrotanum

Ruta graveolens

Vinca minor

Lavandula spica

Stachys lanata

Laburnum alpinum

Sorbus aucuparia

Morus nigra

Liriodendron tulipifera

Taxus baccata 'Fastigiata'

Carpinus betulus

Artemisia arborescens

BIBLIOGRAPHY

Apted, M. R. and Susan Hannabuss. *Painters in Scotland
(1301–1700)*. Edina, Edinburgh (1978).

Bannerman, John. *The Beatons: a Medical Kindred in the Classic
Gaelic Tradition*. John Donald, Edinburgh (1986).

Bown, Deni. *4 Gardens in One*. Royal Botanic Garden/HMSO,
Edinburgh (1992).

Burbridge, Brinsley and Fay Young. *The Royal Botanic Garden
Edinburgh Book of The Scottish Garden*. Moubray House
Publishing, Edinburgh (1989).

Clifford, Derek. *A History of Garden Design*. Faber and Faber,
London (1962).

Connor, Steve. *A Day in the Life of a Medieval Hospital. Independent
on Sunday* (11 July 1993).

Cox, E. H. M. *A History of Gardening in Scotland*. Chatto and
Windus, London (1935).

Genders, Roy. *The Cottage Garden and the Old-Fashioned Flowers*.
Pelham, London (1983).

Gray, M. M. *Scottish Poetry from Barbour to James VI*. J. M. Dent,
London (1935).

Hadfield, Miles. *A History of British Gardening*. John Murray,
London (1979).

Harris, J. *The Artist and the Country House: Garden View Painting in
Britain, 1540–1870*. Southeby Parke Bernat, London (1979).

Hobhouse, Penelope. *Plants in Garden History*. Pavilion, London
(1994).

Howard, Deborah. *Scottish Architecture from the Reformation to the
Restoration, 1560–1660*. Edinburgh University Press,
Edinburgh (1995).

Hynd, Neil. *Towards a Study of Gardening in Scotland from the 16th to
the 18th Centuries. Studies in Scottish Antiquity*, ed. David
Breeze. John Donald, Edinburgh (1984).

Inigo Triggs, H. *Formal Gardens in England and Scotland*. Antique Collector's Club, Woodbridge, Suffolk (1988).

Jamieson, Fiona. *The Royal Gardens of the Palace of Holyrood House 1500–1603. Garden History Society Journal* Vol. 22, no. 1.

Jellicoe, Geoffrey and Susan, Patrick Goode and Michael Lancaster (eds) *The Oxford Companion to Gardens*. Oxford University Press, Oxford (1991).

Justice, James. *The Scots Gardiners Director*. Ruddiman, Edinburgh (1754).

Land Use Consultants, Glasgow. *An Inventory of Gardens and Designed Landscapes in Scotland*. Countryside Commission for Scotland and Historic Buildings and Monuments Directorate of the Scottish Development Department (1987).

Lindsay, Alistair. *The Pleasance of Edzell*. In *Publications of the Clan Lindsay Society*, vol. V, no. 20. Lindsay, Edinburgh (1977).

Lord Lindsay. *Lives of the Lindsays*. John Murray, London (1849).

Lynch, Michael. *A New History of Scotland*. Pimlico, London (1991).

Mabey, Richard and Tony Evans. *The Flowering of Britain*. Hutchinson, London (1980).

McCordick, David (ed.) *Scottish Literature, An Anthology: Volume One*. Peter Lang, New York (1996).

Mackay, Angus. *The Book of Mackay*. Norman Macleod, Edinburgh (1906).

Mackay, Sheila. *Behind the Façade: Four Centuries of Scottish Interiors*. HMSO Edinburgh (1995).

Minay, Priscilla I. M. *James Justice (1698–1763): Eighteenth Century Scots Horticulturalist and Botanist. Garden History Society Journal*, vol. I no. 2, vol. II, no. 2, vol. III, no. 2.

National Galleries of Scotland, Trustees. *Scotland's Pictures*. National Galleries of Scotland, Edinburgh (1990).

National Trust for Scotland:
Culross: A Short Guide to the Royal Burgh. Phil Sked (1981).
Kellie Castle and Garden. Hew Lorimer and Stephanie Blackden (1993). *Pitmedden*. P. Sked, E. Robson and D. Hillson (1984). *The Hermitage* (1997).

Pütter, Jurek. *A Feast of Images: St Andrews' Golden Age 1460–1560*. MacLean Dubois, Edinburgh (1995).

Ramsay, Allan (ed.) *The Evergreen, Vol I*, Allan Ramsay, Edinburgh (1724).

Reid, John. *The Scots Gard'ner*. Published by the author, Edinburgh (1683).

Reid, John. *The Scots Gard'ner*. Introduction by Annette Hope. Mainstream, Edinburgh (1988).

Royal Geographical Society. *The Early Maps of Scotland to 1850: Volume I*. Royal Geographical Society, Edinburgh (1973).

Sanderson, Margaret H. B. *Robert Adam and Scotland: Portrait of an Architect*. HMSO, Edinburgh (1992).

Simpson, W. Douglas. *Edzell Castle*. Historic Scotland/HMSO, Edinburgh (1994).

Spink, William. *Sir John Clerk of Penicuik: Landowner as Designer* in *Furor Hortensis: Essays on the History of the English Landsape Garden*. Elysium, Edinburgh (1974).

Strong, Roy. *The Renaissance Garden in England*. Thames and Hudson, London (1979).

Stuart, David and James Sutherland. *Plants from the Past*. Viking, London (1987).

Sutherland, James. *Hortus Medicus Edinburgensis*. Edinburgh (1683).

Thomson, Duncan. *The Life and Art of George Jamesone*. Clarendon, Oxford (1974).

Yates, Frances A.:

The Valois Tapestries. Warburg Institute, University of London (1959).

The Rosicrucian Enlightenment. Routledge, London and New York (1972).

The Art of Memory. Pimlico, London (1992).

INDEX

COPYRIGHT AND

ACKNOWLEDGEMENTS

Grateful acknowledgement is made to the following sources for permission to reproduce material in this book. Every effort has been made to trace copyright holders, but if any have been inadvertently overlooked the publisher will be pleased to make the necessary arrangement at the first opportunity.

'Northfield House' © The Royal Commission on the Ancient and Historical
    Monuments of Scotland.
'Dean House Panels' – *Sight Personified*, *Taste Personified* and *Hearing Personified*,
    reprinted by permission of the Trustees of the National Museums of Scotland.
'Wagner carpet', Glasgow Museums: Burrell Collection, reproduced by permission.
'Rothiemay Map', from James Gordon's 'Bird's Eye View of Edinburgh' (1647),
    courtesy of Edinburgh City Libraries.
'Middle Eastern Garden', MS Or 338.f.110, by permission of the British Library.
'Ruthven Tapestry' from a bed at Balloch (Taymouth Castle), Glasgow Museums:
    Burrell Collection, reproduced by permission.
'White Lily' from the *Apuleius Platonicus Herbarium*, The Conway Library, Courtauld
    Institute of Art, reproduced by permission of the Provost and Fellows of
    Eton College.
'Master of the Prado Annunciation' (Memling Virgin) by Hans Memling, Glasgow
    Museums: Burrell Collection, reproduced by permission.
'Lion' from the 17th century manuscript *Cosmography* of Zakaria al-Kazwini
    (Yah. Ms. Ar. 1113), Jewish National and University Library, Jerusalem.
'Wild Heilanman' from the Archives of the School of Scottish Studies,
    ref: DII a 6360, reproduced by permission.
'Bee-Boles': Kellie Castle © Brinsley Burbridge, Royal Botanic Garden, Edinburgh.
'Masked Figures' from the *Album Amicorum* of Sir Michael Balfour, reproduced by
    permission of the National Library of Scotland.
Traquair embroidery © The Royal Commission on the Ancient and Historical
    Monuments of Scotland.
'Celestial Ceiling' at Cullen depicting Flora and Mars; by Marc Ellington.
'Mrs Esther Kello' (aka Esther Inglis) by Unknown Artist © The Scottish National
    Portrait Gallery, reproduced with permission.
'Culross – Seal of the Ancient Burgh'/NTS 29. Reprinted by permission of the
    National Trust for Scotland.
Artist's impression of Ingenious Coal Draining Device by Sir George Bruce of
    Culross © National Trust for Scotland.
Illustration of Culross from *Theatrum Scotiae*/*Prospectus Palaty*. Reprinted by
    permission of the National Trust for Scotland.
'Bass Rock' from *Theatrum Scotiae* (1693) by Slezer, reproduced by permission of
    the National Library of Scotland.